Hermann Hesse was born in Germany, at Calw, Württemberg, on 2 July 1877. He began his career as a bookseller and started to write and publish poetry at the age of twenty-one. Five years later he enjoyed his first major success with his novels on youth and educational problems: first *Peter Camenzind* (1904), then *The Prodigy* (1905), followed by *Gertrude* (1910), *Rosshalde* (1914), *Knulp* (1915), and *Demian* (1919). Later, when as a protest against German militarism in the First World War he settled permanently in Switzerland, he established himself as one of the greatest literary figures of the German-speaking world. Hesse's deep humanity and searching philosophy were further developed in such masterly novels as *Siddhartha* (1922), *Steppenwolf* (1927), and *Narziss and Goldmund* (1930), which together with his poems and a number of critical works won him a leading place among contemporary thinkers. In 1946 he won the Nobel Prize for Literature. Hermann Hesse died in 1962 shortly after his eighty-fifth birthday.

Also by Hermann Hesse

Peter Camenzind
The Prodigy
Gertrude
Rosshalde
Knulp
Demian
Strange News from Another Star
Klingsor's Last Summer
Wandering
Siddhartha
Steppenwolf
Narziss and Goldmund
The Journey to the East
The Glass Bead Game
If the War Goes On . . .
Poems
Autobiographical Writings
My Belief
Reflections
Crisis
Stories of Five Decades

Hermann Hesse
A Pictorial Biography

Edited by Volker Michels

Translated by Theodore and Yetta Ziolkowski

Including Hermann Hesse's *Life Story Briefly Told*,
translated by Denver Lindley

TRIAD PANTHER

Published in 1979 by Triad/Panther Books
Frogmore, St Alban's, Herts AL2 2NF
Reprinted 1979

ISBN 0 586 04686 0

Triad Paperbacks Ltd is an imprint of
Chatto, Bodley Head & Jonathan Cape Ltd and
Granada Publishing Ltd

First published in Great Britain by
Triad Paperbacks Ltd 1979
Translation copyright © 1971, 1972, 1975 by
Farrar, Straus and Giroux, Inc.
Translated from the German,
Hermann Hesse: Leben und Werk im Bild
Copyright © Insel Verlag, Frankfurt am Main, 1973
All rights reserved

Made and printed in Great Britain by
Richard Clay (The Chaucer Press) Ltd
Bungay, Suffolk
Set in Monotype Times New Roman

LIFE STORY
BRIEFLY TOLD

I was born toward the end of modern times, shortly before the return of the Middle Ages, with the sign of the Archer on the ascendant and Jupiter in favorable aspect. My birth took place at an early hour of the evening on a warm day in July, and it is the temperature of that hour that I have unconsciously loved and sought throughout my life; when it was lacking I have sorely missed it. I could never live in cold countries and all the voluntary journeys of my life have been directed toward the south. I was the child of pious parents, whom I loved tenderly and would have loved even more tenderly if I had not very early been introduced to the Fourth Commandment. Unfortunately, commandments have always had a disastrous effect on me, however right and well meant they may be—though by nature a lamb and docile as a soap bubble, I have always behaved rebelliously toward commandments of every sort, especially during my youth. All I needed was to hear "thou shalt" and everything in me rose up and I became obdurate. As can be imagined, this peculiarity had a far-reaching and unfortunate effect during my school years. It is true that our teachers taught us, in that amusing subject called world history, that the world has always been governed, guided, and transformed by men who made their own laws and broke with traditional regulations, and we were told that these men should be revered. But this was just as deceitful as all the rest of our instruction, for when one of us, whether with good or bad intent, summoned up courage to protest against some order or even against some silly custom or way of doing things, he was neither revered nor commended as an example but punished instead, made fun of, and crushed by the teachers' dastardly use of their superior power.

Fortunately I had learned even before the beginning of my school years what is most important and valuable in life: I possessed keen, subtle, and finely developed senses which I could rely on and from which I derived great enjoyment, and although later I succumbed irreparably to the enticements of metaphysics and even for a time chastized and neglected my senses, nevertheless a background of tenderly nurtured sensualism, especially in respect to sight and hearing, has always stayed with me and plays a lively part in my intellectual world even when the latter seems abstract. Thus I had provided myself, as I have said, with a certain capacity to meet life long before the beginning of my school years. I knew my way around in the city of my fathers, in the barnyards and in the forests, in the truck gardens and in the workshops of the mechanics; I knew trees, birds, and butterflies, I could sing songs and whistle through my teeth and much else besides that is important for living. To this was now added various sorts of school knowledge, which came easy to me and gave me pleasure; in particular I got real enjoyment from the Latin language and I was writing Latin verses almost as soon as German ones. For the art of lying and of diplomacy I have my second year in school to thank, during which a preceptor and his accomplice afforded me mastery of these accomplishments after I had earlier brought down upon myself in my childish openness and trustfulness one disaster after another. These two educators successfully opened my eyes to the fact that a sense of humor and a love of truth were not qualities they were looking for in pupils. They ascribed to me a misdeed, a quite unimportant one which had occurred in class and of which I was wholly innocent, and since they could not force me to confess that I was the culprit, the trivial matter was turned into an inquisition and the two tortured and beat out of me, not the desired confession, to be sure, but instead all belief in the decency of the teaching profession. In time, thank God, I became acquainted with teachers worthy of respect, but the damage had been done, and my relations not only with schoolmasters but with all authority were distorted and embittered. On the whole I was a good student during my first seven or eight years in school; at any rate I regularly stood among the first in my class. It was not until those battles began which no one who is going to become a person is spared that I came more and more into conflict with the school. Two decades were to pass before I understood those battles; at the time they were simply going on all around me, contrary to my will, and were a great misery.

The thing was this: from my thirteenth year on, it was clear to me that I wanted to be either a poet or nothing at all. To this realization, however, was gradually added a further, painful insight. One could become a teacher, minister, doctor, mechanic, merchant, post-office employee, or a musician, painter, architect; there was a path to every profession in the world, there were prerequisites, a school, a course of instruction for the beginner. Only for the poet there was nothing of the sort! It was permissible and even considered an honor to be a poet; that is, to be successful and famous as a poet—unfortunately by that time one was usually dead. But to become a poet was impossible, and to want to become one was ridiculous and shameful, as I very soon found out. I had quickly learned what there was to be learned from the situation: a poet was simply something you were allowed to be but not to become. Further: native poetic talent and interest in poetry were suspect in teachers' eyes; you were either distrusted for it or ridiculed, often, indeed, subjected to deadly insults. With the poet it was exactly the same as with the hero, and with all strong, handsome, high-spirited, non-commonplace figures and enterprises: in the past they were magnificent, every school book was filled with their praises; in the present, in real life, people hated them, and presumably teachers were especially selected and trained to prevent as far as possible the rise of magnificent, free human beings and the accomplishment of great and splendid deeds.

Thus I saw between me and my distant goal nothing but abysses yawning; everything was uncertain, everything devoid of value, only one thing remained constant: that I intended to become a poet, whether that turned out to be easy or hard, ridiculous or creditable. The external consequences of this resolve —or rather of this fatality—were as follows.

When I was thirteen years old and this conflict had just begun, my conduct in my parents' house as well as in school left so much to be desired that I was banished to a Latin school in another city. A year later I became a pupil in a theological seminary, learned to write the Hebrew alphabet, and was already on the point of grasping what a *dagesh forte implicitum* is, when suddenly from inside me storms arose that led to flight from the monastery school, punishment by strict imprisonment, and dismissal from the seminary.

Then for a while I struggled to advance my studies at a Gymnasium; however, the lock-up and expulsion were the end there too. After that, for three days I was a merchant's apprentice, ran away again, and for several days and nights, to the great distress of my parents, disappeared. For a period of six months I was my father's assistant, for a year and a half I was an employee in a mechanical workshop and tower-clock factory.

In short, for more than four years everything that was attempted with me went wrong; no school would keep me, in no course of instruction did I last for long. Every attempt to make a useful human being out of me ended in failure, several times in shame and scandal, in flight or expulsion, and yet everywhere they admitted that I had ability and even a reasonable amount of determination! Also I was nothing if not industrious—the high virtue of idleness I have always regarded with awe, but I have never mastered it. In my sixteenth year, after my school career had ended in failure, I consciously and energetically began my own education, and it was my good fortune and delight that in my father's house was my grandfather's huge library, a whole hall full of old books, which contained among other things all of eighteenth-century German literature and philosophy. Between my sixteenth and twentieth years I not only covered a quantity of paper with my first attempts at poetry but I also read half of the world's literature and applied myself to the history of art, languages, and philosophy with a persistence that would have abundantly sufficed for any normal college career.

Then I became a bookseller in order finally to earn my own bread. I had always been on better terms with books than with the vises and cogwheels with which I had tortured myself as a mechanic. At first, swimming in modern, indeed the most modern, literature and in fact being overwhelmed by it was an almost intoxicating joy. But after a while I noticed that in matters of the spirit, a life simply in the present, in the modern and most modern, is unbearable and meaningless, that the life of the spirit is made possible only by constant reference to what is past, to history, to the ancient and primeval. And so after that first joy was exhausted it became a necessity for me to return from my submersion in novelties to what is old; this I accomplished by moving from the bookshop to an antique shop. However, I only stuck to this profession for as long as I needed it to sustain life. At the age of twenty-six, as a result of my first literary success, I gave it up too.

Thus, amid so many storms and sacrifices, my goal had now been reached: however impossible it may have appeared, I had become a poet and had, it would seem, won the long, stubborn battle with the world. The bitterness of my years of schooling and preparation, during which I had often been very close to ruin, was now forgotten or laughed at— even my relations and friends, who had previously been in despair about me, now smiled encouragingly. I had triumphed, and now if I did the silliest or most trivial thing it was thought charming, just as I was greatly charmed by myself. Now for the first time I realized in what dreadful isolation, asceticism, and danger I had lived year after year; the warm breeze of recognition did me good and I began to be a contented man.

Outwardly my life now ran on for a good while in calm and agreeable fashion. I had a wife, children, a house and garden. I wrote my books, I was considered an amiable poet, and I lived at peace with the world. In the year 1905 I helped to found a periodical which was principally directed against the personal government of Wilhelm II, without myself taking this political aim very seriously. I took interesting trips in Switzerland, Germany, Austria, Italy, India. Everything seemed to be in order.

Then came the summer of 1914, and suddenly everything looked different, inwardly and outwardly. It became evident that our former well-being had rested on insecure foundations, and accordingly there now began a period of misery, the great education. The so-called time of testing had come, and I cannot say that it found me better prepared, worthier, or superior to anyone else. What distinguished me from others at that time was only that I lacked the great compensation so many others possessed: enthusiasm. For that reason I came to myself again and into conflict with my environment. I was once more put to school, had to unlearn my satisfaction with myself and with the world, and in this experience I stepped for the first time over the threshold of initiation into life.

I have never forgotten a little encounter during the first year of the war. I had gone to visit a large military hospital in the hope of finding a way of fitting myself in some meaningful fashion into the altered world—something that still seemed possible to me at that time. In that hospital for the wounded, I met an elderly spinster who had formerly lived on a private income in comfortable circumstances and was now serving as a nurse in the wards. She told me with touching enthusiasm how happy and proud she was to have been allowed to witness this great time. I found that understandable, for in this lady's case it had taken the war to transform her indolent and purely egotistical old maid's existence into an active and useful life. But as she expressed her happiness to me in a corridor full of bandaged and shell-crippled soldiers, between wards that were full of amputees and dying men, my heart turned over. Well though I understood Auntie's enthusiasm, I could not share it, I could not commend it. If for every ten wounded men such another enthusiastic nurse came along, then these ladies' happiness cost too much.

No, I could not share the joy over the great time, and so it came about that from the beginning I suffered miserably from the war, and for a period of years strove in desperation to protect myself against a misfortune that had seemed to fall upon me out of a clear blue sky, while everybody around me acted as though they were full of happy enthusiasm over this same misery. And when I read newspaper articles by prominent writers in which they disclosed the blessings of the war, and the clarion call of the professors, and all the war poems issuing from the studies of famous poets, then I became more wretched still.

One day in 1915 a public confession of this wretchedness escaped me, together with an expression of regret that even so-called spiritual people could find nothing better to do than preach hatred, spread lies, and praise the great misfortune to the skies. The result of this rather hesitantly expressed lament was that in the press of my native land I was denounced as a traitor—a new experience for me since despite many contacts with the press I had never before been spat at by the majority. The article containing this denunciation was printed by twenty papers in my country, and of all the friends I thought I had among newspaper men only two dared rise to my defense. Old friends informed me that they had been nurturing a viper in their bosoms and that those bosoms in future would throb only for Kaiser and for Reich and not for a degenerate like me. Abusive letters from strangers came in stacks, and the bookdealers gave me to understand that an author with such reprehensible views has ceased to exist so far as they were concerned. On a number of these letters I came to recognize a decoration which I saw then for the first time: a little round stamp with the inscription *God punish England.*

One might think that I would have had a hearty laugh at this misunderstanding. But I could do nothing of the sort. This experience, unimportant in itself, brought me as reward the second great transformation of my life.

The first transformation, you recall, took place at the instant when I recognized my determination to become a poet. The hitherto model pupil Hesse became from then on a bad pupil: he was punished, expelled, he did nothing right, he caused himself and his parents one worry after another—all simply because he saw no possibility of reconciliation between the world as it happens to be or seems to be and the voice of his own heart. Once more I saw myself in conflict with a world with which I had until then been living in complete content. Once more everything went awry for me, once more I was alone and miserable, once more everything I said and thought was deliberately misinterpreted by others. Once more, between reality and what seemed to me good, desirable, and sensible, I saw a hopeless abyss yawning.

This time, however, I was not spared a self-examination. Before long I found myself obliged to seek the cause of my sufferings not outside but inside myself. For this much at least I could clearly see: to accuse the whole world of delusion and brutality was something no human being and no god had a right to do, I least of all. And so there must be all sorts of disorder in me if I was in such sharp conflict with the whole course of the world. And behold, there was in fact a great disorder. It was no pleasure to come to grips with that disorder in myself and try to transform it into order. One thing became clear at once: the benign content in which I had lived with the world had not only been bought at too high a price; it had been just as corrupt as the outer peace of the world. I had believed that through the long, hard battles of youth I had earned my place in the world and that I was now a poet. Meanwhile, success and prosperity had had their usual effect on me, I had become complacent and comfortable, and when I looked carefully the poet was hardly to be distinguished from a writer of cheap fiction. Things had gone too well with me. Now, though, abundant provision was made for heavy going, which is always a good and salutary training, and so I learned more and more to let the business of the world go its way, and I could concern myself with my own share in the confusion and guilt of the whole. To detect this concern in my writings is something I must leave to the reader. And yet I always retained the secret hope that in time my people too, not as a whole but through many alert and responsible individuals, would successfully pass through a similar testing, and in place of laments and curses at the wicked war and the wicked enemy and the wicked revolution, in a thousand hearts the question would arise: How have I myself become a party to this guilt?

And how can I regain my innocence? For one can always regain one's innocence if one acknowledges one's suffering and guilt and suffers to the end instead of trying to lay the blame on others.

As this new transformation began to express itself in my writings and in my life, many of my friends shook their heads. Many, too, abandoned me. That was a part of the altered pattern of my life, just like the loss of my house, my family, and other goods and comforts. It was a time when I daily said goodbye and was daily astounded that I was now able to bear this too and still go on living and still find something to love in this strange existence that seemed, really, to bring me only pain, disillusionment, and loss.

However, to make up for this, I had even during the war years something like a good star or guardian angel. While I felt myself very much alone with my suffering and, until the beginning of the transformation, hourly felt my fate as accursed and execrated it, my very suffering and my obsession with suffering served me as shield and buckler against the outside world. I spent the war years, in fact, in such horrible circumstances of politics, espionage, bribery, and corruption as even at that time were rarely to be found concentrated in one place, namely in Bern, amid German, neutral, and hostile diplomacy, in a city that had been flooded overnight by a tidal wave of diplomats, secret agents, spies, journalists, speculators, and profiteers. I lived amid diplomats and soldiers, had contacts with people from many enemy countries, the air around me was a single net of espionage and counterespionage, of intrigue, denunciations, and political and personal speculation —and of all this in all those years I noticed nothing at all! I was shadowed, listened to, spied upon; I was an object of suspicion now to the enemy, now to the neutrals, now to my own countrymen, and I noticed none of it. Only long afterward did I learn this and that about it, and I could not understand how I had been able to live enveloped in this atmosphere, untouched and unharmed. But that is what happened.

With the end of the war there coincided the completion of my transformation and the climax of suffering in my trial. This suffering no longer had anything to do with the war or the fate of the world; even the defeat of Germany, which we abroad had foreseen with certainty for two years, was at that time no longer terrifying. I was wholly immersed in myself and in my own fate, though at times with the feeling that the lot of mankind was involved as well. I found reflected in myself all the world's lust for war and murder, all its irresponsibility, all its gross self-indulgence, all its cowardice; I had to lose first my self-respect and then my self-contempt; I had no less a task than to carry through to the end my scrutiny of chaos, with the now soaring, now sinking hope of rediscovering, beyond chaos, nature and innocence. Every human being who has been awakened and really has achieved consciousness has on one or more occasions walked this narrow path through the wilderness—to try to talk to others about it would be a fruitless effort.

When friends were disloyal to me, I sometimes felt sadness but never disgust; I felt this rather as a reassurance on my way. Those former friends were surely right when they said that once I had been so sympathetic as a man and a poet, whereas my present problematic attitude was simply unbearable. In questions of taste and of character I had long since passed beyond them; there was no one among them to whom my vocabulary would have been comprehensible. These friends were perhaps right when they reproached me with having lost beauty and harmony in my writing. Such words simply made me laugh—what is beauty or harmony to one who is condemned to death, who is running for his life between collapsing walls? Perhaps, too, my lifelong belief notwithstanding, I was not a poet, and the whole aesthetic impulse had simply been a mistake? Why not? Even that was no longer of any importance. Most of what I had been confronted with in the course of the journey through the hell of myself had been false and worthless, and perhaps this was also the case with the illusion of my vocation or gift. How unimportant that was, after all! And that which once, full of pride and childish joy, I had regarded as my task was no longer there either. I saw my task, or rather my way of salvation, no longer in the realm of lyric poetry or philosophy or any one of the occupations of specialists but rather simply in letting what little there was in me that was vital and strong live its life, simply in unqualified loyalty now to what I felt to be still alive within myself. That was Life, that was God. —Afterward, when such times of high, mortally dangerous exaltation are passed, all this looks strangely different, because the former contents of consciousness and their names are now without meaning, and what was holy the day before yesterday can sound almost comic.

When the war finally came to an end for me too, in the spring of 1919, I withdrew into a remote corner of Switzerland and became a hermit. Because all my life I had been much occupied with Indian and Chinese wisdom (this was an inheritance from my parents and grandparents), and also because I gave my new experiences expression in part in the picture language of the East, I was often called a "Buddhist." At this I could only laugh, for at bottom I knew of no religion from which I was further removed. And yet there was something accurate, a grain of truth hidden in this, which I first recognized somewhat later. If it were in any way thinkable that a person should choose a religion for himself, then I should certainly out of inner longing have joined a conservative religion: Confucianism, Brahmanism, or the Roman Church. I should have done this, however, out of longing for my polar opposite, not from innate affinity, for it was not by accident alone that I was born the son of pious Protestants; I am a Protestant by temperament and nature as well (to which my deep antipathy to the present Protestant denominations is no contradiction whatever). For the true Protestant is in opposition to his own church just as he is to every other, since his nature constrains him to affirm becoming above being. And in this sense Buddha, too, was certainly a Protestant.

My belief in my vocation as poet and in the value of my literary labors had thus been uprooted since the transformation. Writing no longer gave me any real joy. But a human being must have some joy; even in the midst of my distress I asserted that claim. I could renounce Justice, Reason, Meaning in life and in the world; I had seen that the world could get along splendidly without these abstractions—but I could not get along without some bit of joy, and the demand for that bit of joy was now one of those little flames inside me in which I still believed, and from which I planned to create the world anew for myself. Often I sought my joy, my dream, my forgetfulness in a bottle of wine, and very often it was of help; praised be it therefor. But it was not enough. And then, behold, one day I discovered an entirely new joy. Suddenly, at the age of forty, I began to paint. Not that I considered myself a painter or intended to become one. But painting is marvelous; it makes one happier and more patient. Afterward one does not have black fingers as with writing but red and blue ones. At this painting, too, many of my friends have taken offense. I don't have much luck that way—whenever I undertake something very necessary, auspicious, and beautiful, people become cross. They would like one to stay as one is; they don't want one's face to change. But my face will not conform! It insists on changing often; that's a necessity.

Another reproach thrown at me seems to me fully justified. People say that I have no sense of reality. The poems I write as well as the little pictures I paint do not correspond with reality. When I write I frequently forget the demands that cultivated readers make of a proper book, and more important still, I really do lack respect for reality. I consider reality to be the last thing one need concern oneself about, for it is, tediously enough, always present, while more beautiful and necessary things demand our attention and care. Reality is what one must not under any circumstances be satisfied with, what one must not under any circumstances worship and revere, for it is accidental, the offal of life. And it is in no wise to be changed, this shabby, consistently disappointing and barren reality, except by our denying it and proving in the process that we are stronger than it is.

In my writings people often miss the customary respect for reality, and when I paint, the trees have faces and the houses laugh or dance or weep, but whether the tree is a pear or chestnut, that for the most part cannot be determined. I must accept this reproach. I admit that my own life frequently appears to me exactly like a legend, I often see and feel the outer world connected and in harmony with my inner world in a way that I can only call magical.

A few more absurd occurrences befell me. For example, I once made a harmless observation about the famous poet Schiller, whereupon all the South German bowling clubs denounced me as a desecrator of the sacred relics of the fatherland. Now, however, for a number of years I have succeeded in not saying anything to desecrate relics or make people get red with rage. I consider this an improvement.

Now since so-called reality plays no very important role for me, since the past often occupies me as if it were the present, and the present seems to me infinitely far away, for these reasons I cannot separate the future from the past as sharply as is usually done. I live a great deal in the future and so I need not end my biography with the present day but can let it go quietly on.

I shall give a brief account of how my life completes its curve. In the years up to 1930 I wrote a few more books, only then to turn my back on that profession forever. The question whether or not I was really to be counted among the poets was investigated in two dissertations by diligent young people, but not answered. It transpired, in fact, as the result of a careful examination of modern literature that the aura which distinguishes the poet has become in modern times so very attenuated that the distinction between poets and men of letters can no longer be made. From this objective state of affairs, however, the two Ph.D. candidates drew opposite conclusions. One of them, the more sympathetic, was of the opinion that poesy in such ridiculous attenuation was poetry no longer, and since plain literature is not worth keeping alive, one might as well let what is still called poetry quietly pass away. The other, however, was an unqualified admirer of poesy, even in its flimsiest form, and therefore he believed it was better to admit a hundred non-poets as insurance rather than wrong a single poet who might perhaps still have a drop of the genuine blood of Parnassus in his veins.

I was principally occupied with painting and with Chinese magic spells, but in the following years became more and more absorbed in music. It was the ambition of my later life to write a sort of opera in which human life in its so-called reality would be viewed with scant seriousness, ridiculed, in fact; in its eternal value, however, it would shine forth as image and momentary vesture of the Godhead. The magical conception of life had always been close to my heart, I had never been a "modern man," and had always considered Von Hoffmann's "Pot of

Gold" and even *Heinrich von Ofterdingen* more valuable textbooks than any natural history or history of the world. (In point of fact, whenever I read any of the latter I always looked upon them as delightful fables.) But now I had entered upon that period of life in which it no longer makes sense to continue elaborating and differentiating a personality that is already complete and more than adequately differentiated, in which instead the task becomes that of allowing the estimable I to disappear once more into the universe and, in the face of mutability, to take one's place in the eternal and timeless order. To express these thoughts or attitudes toward life seemed to me possible only by means of fairy tales, and I looked upon the opera as the highest form of fairy tale, presumably because I could no longer really believe in the magic of the word in our ill-used and dying speech, whereas magic continued to seem to me a living tree on whose branches apples of paradise might grow even today. In my opera I wanted to do what I had never quite succeeded in doing in my poetry: to establish a high and delightful meaning for human life. I wanted to praise the innocence and inexhaustibility of nature and to present her course up to that point where, through inevitable suffering, she is forced to turn toward spirit, her distant polar opposite, and the oscillation of life between these two poles of nature and of spirit would be revealed as blithe, playful, and complete as the arch of a rainbow.

However, I was never, alas, successful in completing that opera. My experience with it was the same as with my poetry. I had had to give the latter up after I had seen that everything that seemed to me important to say had already been said a thousand times more clearly in "Pot of Gold" and in *Heinrich von Ofterdingen* than I was able to say it. And that is the way it now went with my opera. Just when I had completed my years of preparatory

musical studies and had made several drafts of the
text and was once more trying to visualize as pene-
tratingly as possible the real meaning and content of
my work, just then I had a sudden realization that
in my opera I was attempting exactly the same thing
that had been so magnificently accomplished long
before in *The Magic Flute*.

I therefore laid this work aside and now devoted
myself entirely to practical magic. If my dream of
being an artist had been an illusion, if I was in-
capable of a "Pot of Gold" or a *Magic Flute*, at least
I was a born magician. By the Eastern path of Lao-
tse and the I Ching, I had long ago advanced far
enough to know with certainty about the accidental
nature and mutability of so-called reality. Now
through magic I manipulated this reality according
to my wishes and I must say I took much joy in
doing so. I have to confess, however, that I did not
always confine myself to the noble garden known as
white magic, but from time to time was drawn over
to the black side by that lively little flame within me.

At the age of more than seventy, just after two
universities had singled me out for honorary degrees,
I was brought to trial for the seduction by magic of
a young girl. In jail I begged for permission to pass
the time by painting. This was granted. Friends
brought me paints and artist's materials, and I
painted a little landscape on the wall of my cell.
Thus I had once more returned to art, and all the
shipwrecks I had suffered as an artist could not
deter me for a moment from draining once more
that noblest of cups, from building up once again
like a child at play a lovely little play world, and
from sating my heart with it, from once more throw-
ing away all wisdom and abstraction and turning to
the primitive lust of creation. Thus I was painting
once more, I was mixing colors and dipping brushes
in them, drinking in again with enchantment all
that endless magic: the bright, happy sound of

cinnabar, the full, clear note of yellow, the deep, moving tone of blue, and the music of their mixture out to the furthest, palest gray. Happy as a child, I carried on this game of creation and so painted the landscape on the wall of my cell. This landscape contained almost everything that had given me pleasure in life: rivers and mountains, sea and clouds, peasants at harvest time, and a crowd of other beautiful things in which I had taken joy. But in the middle of the picture there ran a very small railroad train. It was going straight toward the mountain and its head was already buried in it like a worm in an apple, the locomotive had already entered a little tunnel out of whose dark mouth sooty smoke was pouring.

Never before had my play enchanted me as it did this time. In my return to art I forgot not only that I was a prisoner, an accused man with little prospect of ending my life anywhere save in a penitentiary—I even frequently forgot my magical exercises and seemed to myself magician enough when I created with my thin brush a tiny tree, a small bright cloud.

Meanwhile, so-called reality, with which I now had in fact completely fallen out, was at great pains to make fun of my dream and to shatter it again and again. Almost every day I was led under guard into extremely uncongenial chambers where amid many papers unsympathetic men sat and questioned me, refused to believe me, barked at me, threatened me now like a three-year-old child and now like a hardened criminal. One doesn't need to be accused in order to become acquainted with this remarkable and truly hellish business of courts, papers, and ordinances. Of all the hells that men have so strangely had to create for themselves, this has always seemed to me the most hellish. All you need to do is to plan to move or to marry, to request a passport or a certificate of citizenship, and you find yourself at once in the midst of this hell; you have to spend bitter hours in the airless space of this paper world, you are questioned by bored yet hurried, disgruntled men, snapped at, you are met by disbelief for the simplest, truest statement, you are treated now like a schoolchild, now like a criminal. Well, everyone knows this. I should long since have been smothered and desiccated in this paper hell if it had not been that my paints constantly comforted and revived me and my picture, my beautiful little landscape, gave me renewed air and life.

It was in front of this picture in my cell that I was standing one day when the guards came hurrying up once more with their tedious summons and tried to tear me away from my happy activity. At that moment I felt weariness and something like revulsion against all this bustle, this whole brutal and spiritless reality. It seemed to me high time to put an end to my torment. If I was not allowed to play my innocent artist's game undisturbed, then I must have recourse to those sterner arts to which I had devoted so many years of my life. Without magic this world was unbearable.

I called to mind the Chinese formula, stood for a minute with suspended breath, and freed myself from the illusion of reality. I then affably requested the guards to be patient for a moment longer since I had to step into my picture and look after something in the train. They laughed in their usual way, for they considered me mentally unbalanced.

Then I made myself small and stepped into my picture, got aboard the little train, and rode in the little train into the little black tunnel. For a while sooty smoke continued to be visible, pouring out of the round hole, then the smoke dispersed and disappeared and with it the entire picture and I with the picture.

The guards remained behind in great embarrassment.

(1925)

CALW

1 Calw in the Black Forest, Hermann Hesse's birth-
place, where he spent the first three years of his life
(until 1881), and to which he returned to attend school
for three years (1886–9). The Gothic chapel of St.
Nicholas on the old bridge over the Nagold:
"Only the old stone bridge with its Gothic chapel serves
as a reminder that the modest and industrious little
village is more than two centuries old." (From Hesse's
"Calw diary," 1901)

2 The Hesse family in the year 1889. Left to right:
Hermann, his father, Marulla, his mother, Adele, and
Hans

A

MALAYALAM AND ENGLISH

DICTIONARY.

ആ

A

3 Dr. Carl Hermann Hesse (1802–96), paternal grandfather, physician in Weissenstein, Estonia

4 From the large Malayalam dictionary, which Hermann Gundert worked on for thirty years

5 Dr. Hermann Gundert (1814–93), maternal grandfather, missionary, linguist; head of the Calw Publishing House

6 Marie Hesse (1842–1902), née Gundert, widow of the missionary Karl Isenberg; Hesse's mother

7 Johannes Hesse (1847–1916), missionary and later head of the Calw Publishing House; Hesse's father

8 Hermann Hesse at the age of four

9 The Mission School in Basel, where the Hesse family lived from 1881–6. Hermann spent his first school years here: "In 1880 my father was called to Basel, where he was a teacher at the Mission School. At first, he remained a Russian citizen, but later he acquired citizenship, so that, as a young boy, I became a citizen of Switzerland and Basel. Then, however, my father was called back to Calw in 1886 to work as the associate of and later as the successor to my grandfather. The other members of the family retained their Basel and Swiss citizenship, but, since I would be studying in Württemberg and taking the state examinations there, I alone was registered for naturalization in 1890 by my parents. The petition was granted, and I became a citizen of Württemberg. Later I paid for that the hard way with four years' service in the war and other sacrifices"

10 The building (first house on the left) which housed
the bookstore of the Calw Publishing House, where the
Hesse family resided from 1886–9 and after 1893. This is
the setting for *Demian, A Child's Soul,* and other
stories

11 The marketplace in Calw. In the background is the
house where Hesse was born

12 The Calw Grammar School, which was the setting for
many stories, among them "The Interrupted Class"

13 Hermann Hesse, 1895: "I was in most respects intellectually precocious, began to write verses at a very early age, about age six. . . . From my twelfth year on, it was my desire and goal to become a writer, and since there was no normal route to this, I had much difficulty because of my choice of a profession"

14 Hesse's sisters, Marulla (left) and Adele

15 The former Calw Poorhouse, described in the story "In the Old Sun" (1903)

MAULBRONN

16/17 The former Cistercian Abbey at Maulbronn, since
1565 a Protestant seminary. Boys from ages ten to
fourteen received free preparatory schooling here before
they began the study of Protestant theology:
"It was taken for granted, in view of family tradition
and my promise, that I would continue my studies,
and that they would be in theology. This not only
fulfilled the wish of the family, but it was also the
most economical. For theology students in
Württemberg, a free education was available to all
boys from age fourteen on who had successfully
passed the regional examinations"

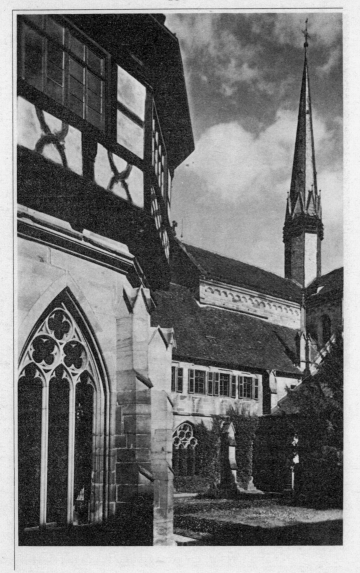

18 Maulbronn, the background for many stories

19 The fountain in the cloister at Maulbronn

20 Class VII of the Gymnasium in Bad Cannstatt in 1893. In the middle of the back row, Hermann Hesse

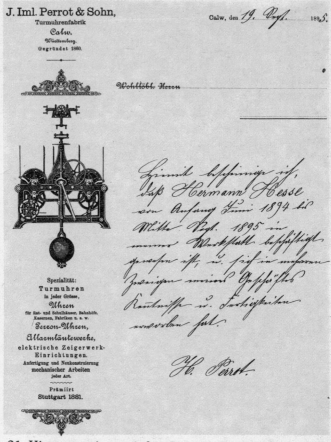

J. Iml. Perrot & Sohn,
Turmuhrenfabrik
Calw.
Württemberg.
Gegründet 1860.

Calw, den *19. Sept.* 189*5*.

Wohllöbl. Herren

Hiermit bescheinige ich, daß Hermann Hesse von Anfang Juni 1894 bis Mitte Sept. 1895 in meiner Werkstatt beschäftigt gewesen ist, u. sich in unseren Zweigen meines Geschäfts Kenntnisse u. Fertigkeiten erworben hat.

H. Perrot.

Spezialität:
Turmuhren
in jeder Grösse,
Uhren
für Rat- und Schulhäuser, Bahnhöfe,
Kasernen, Fabriken u. s. w.
Perron-Uhren,
Allarmläutewerke,
elektrische Zeigerwerk-
Einrichtungen.
Anfertigung und Neukonstruierung
mechanischer Arbeiten
jeder Art.

Prämiirt
Stuttgart 1881.

21 His apprentice period in Perrot's Clockworks Factory in Calw lasted from June 5, 1894, to September 19, 1895. (See such stories as *Beneath the Wheel*, "From the Workshop," "Hans Dierlamm's Apprenticeship," "The First Adventure"): "Despite the fact that I had absolutely no talent and no interest in technical and mechanical work, and realized almost immediately that in this profession I could never be successful, I remained with it long enough to learn a great deal. For the first and only time in my life I lived in close contact with working-class people"

TÜBINGEN

22 Tübingen at the end of the nineteenth century, where
the nineteen-year-old Hesse began his four-year bookdealer's apprenticeship on October 4, 1895

23 The twenty-one-year-old bookdealer's apprentice in
Tübingen: "There I struggled through the three-year apprenticeship, which was anything but easy, and
remained another year as the youngest employee in the
store, with a salary of eighty marks monthly. During
this time I read much and did my first writing. Of these
efforts only *Hermann Lauscher* survives, which in part
actually originated in Basel, as well as the *Romantic
Songs* and *An Hour Beyond Midnight* (both 1899). In
the early Tübingen period I was very industrious and
dependable; later I caroused around a lot with the
students (see *Hermann Lauscher*), but nonetheless
performed my job well. The first few years in my
private studies I was almost completely preoccupied
with Goethe, with his writings and his life. This cult
was replaced around 1897 or 1898 by a cult of
Nietzsche"

24 The marketplace in Tübingen

25 Julie Hellmann ("Lulu" in *Hermann Lauscher*), whom Hesse and his friends of the *Petit cénacle* met in the summer of 1899 in Kirchheim/Teck

26 The *Petit cénacle* (from left to right: Otto Erich Faber, Oskar Rupp, Ludwig Finckh, Carlo Hammelehle, Hesse)

> Wir galten als dekadent und modern
> Und glaubten es mit Behagen.
> Im Wirklichkeit waren wir junge Herrn
> Von höchst modestem Betragen.
>> ("Dem Petit cénacle")

> We were considered decadent and modern
> And we believed it complacently.
> In reality we were young gentlemen
> Of extremely modest demeanor.
>> ("To the Petit Cénacle")

27 Heckenhauer Bookshop in Tübingen, at the time of
Hesse's apprenticeship

28 The first published work, *Romantic Songs*, partially
financed by the author, with the Dresden vanity press
of E. Pierson, where previously such well-known authors
as Arthur Schnitzler and Hermann Bahr had made their
debut. The booklet appeared in the fall of 1898 (bearing
the date 1899) in an edition of six hundred copies

Romantische Lieder

Von

Hermann Hesse.

Hermann Hesse
Eine Stunde hinter
Mitternacht.

29 Rainer Maria Rilke as a young man: "He was the
only one, in the year 1899, who wrote a favorable
word about my *An Hour Beyond Midnight.* His
entire oeuvre belongs to the best that Germany, which
is not very rich spiritually, has produced in the last
twenty-five years." (Letter, 1931)

30 First prose publication of Hesse's *An Hour Beyond
Midnight,* which appeared in 1899, Eugen Diederichs
Publishers, arranged through the mediation of the
popular novelist Helen Voigt, who had been in
correspondence with Hesse since 1897

31 Helene Voigt (1875–1961). Studio portrait which
she sent to Hesse in Tübingen, May 1898

BASEL

S. FISCHER, VERLAG, BERLIN W., BÜLOWSTRASSE 91.

Herrn H. Hesse   Basel
++++++++++

BERLIN W., DEN 30/1. 03.

Sehr geehrter Herr !

Wir haben mit grossem Vergnügen die hinterlassenen Gedichte und Schriften von Hermann Lauscher gelesen und steht viel Schönes auf diesen wenigen Seiten und eine nicht gemeine Hoffnung knüpft sich daran an. Es würde uns freuen, wenn Sie uns neuere Arbeiten von Ihnen mitteilen wollten.

Mit vorzüglicher Hochachtung

S. Fischer Verlag

S. FISCHER, VERLAG, BERLIN W., BÜLOWSTRASSE 91.

BERLIN W., DEN 9/5 1903

Sehr geehrter Herr!

Ich bin sehr erfreut zu hören, dass Sie mir Ihr neues Werk senden und ich will mir gleich sagen: ich erwarte es mit Spannung. Seien Sie versichert, dass ich gleich nach Eintreffen der Sendung an die Lecture gehe und dass ich nicht säumen werde, Sie von meinem Eindruck zu verständigen.

Mit Hochachtungsvollen Grüssen

Ihr ergebener

Fischer

32/33 The first two letters (both dated 1903) to Hesse
from the publisher S. Fischer, who expressed an
interest in considering future manuscripts by the still
unknown young writer; his encouragement prompted
Hesse to submit his next work, *Peter Camenzind*

34 View of the Old City in Basel, where Hesse, on
September 15, 1899, began work as a stock clerk in the
Reich'sche Buchhandlung. In the press connected
with this bookdealer, he published "for his friends and
those who are well-disposed toward him" the *Posthumous
Writings and Poems of Hermann Lauscher,* which
brought Hesse to the attention of the publisher S. Fischer

35 Jakob Burckhardt (1818–97), Swiss cultural historian. In Basel, Hesse lived "in the midst of a circle of people whose knowledge and interests, whose readings and travels, whose mode of thought, conception of history, and conversation were influenced and shaped by nothing and no one so strongly as by Jakob Burckhardt." (*Basel Reminiscences*)

36 Hesse at the time of the writing of *Peter Camenzind:*
"If independence, incorruptibility of conscience
are still valid ideals for intellectual achievement, our age
is indebted for this to such exemplary spirits as
Burckhardt." (Hesse, 1935, in a review)

37 The publisher Samuel Fischer (1859–1934)

38 Dust jacket of the first edition of *Peter Camenzind*,
1904

39 Walther Rathenau (1867–1922), German statesman
and industrialist. Among the first reviewers of the book
were Stefan Zweig and Walther Rathenau, who reviewed it in the same year under the heading "A Good
Book." In a letter to Hesse in 1918, Rathenau wrote:
"The first and only book review which I have ever written
. . . concerned your book *Peter Camenzind*. The editor
thought at the time that it was of service to the book,
and I hope this was the case"

40/41 In Calw, influenced by two trips to Italy (1901 and 1903), Hesse wrote the biographical studies *Boccaccio* (February 1904) and *Francis of Assisi* (May 1904), which were published in the same year. Books designed by Heinrich Vogeler, a fashionable German artist

GAIENHOFEN

42 "At the time I was in Calw with my father and sisters
writing *Beneath the Wheel*, my wife discovered the
village of Gaienhofen in Baden on Lake Constance,
and in it was an unoccupied peasant house on a quiet
square across from the village chapel." On August 10,
1904, Hesse moved to this house, where he lived for
three years

43 Boat dock in Gaienhofen with Hesse's rowboat in the
foreground: "There are no people of culture here, also
no conveniences at all; in fact, I must obtain almost all
my groceries by rowboat from the nearest town
[Steckborn in Switzerland]." (Letter, 1904)

44 Maria (called Mia) Hesse, née Bernoulli (1868–1963), mother of Hesse's three sons

45 Hesse in Gaienhofen around 1909

46 With his oldest son, Bruno, on Lake Constance in
Gaienhofen

47 The house which Hesse built in Gaienhofen in 1907,
Am Erlenloh

48 Drinking chianti in Fiesole, 1906

> Man warnt vor dem Beruf des Dichters
> Auch vor dem Flöten, Trommeln, Geigen
> Weil Leute ähnlichen Gelichters
> So oft zu Trunk und Leichtsinn neigen.

> People warn you against the profession of poet,
> Also against playing the flute, the drums, the violin,
> Because riffraff of this sort
> So often tend toward drinking and frivolity.
> (From Hesse's unpublished light verse)

49/50/51 The stories (*Beneath the Wheel, In This World, Neighbors*) written in Calw and Gaienhofen, which appeared in 1906, 1907, and 1908

52 Theodor Heuss (1884–1963) as a young man. Heuss was a journalist and professor and President of the Federal Republic of Germany from 1949 to 1959. After publication of *Hermann Lauscher* he followed the appearance of each new work by Hesse and reviewed many of them, including *The Glass Bead Game*. He published reviews of each of these three story collections: "The generations of youth now coming of age will sense the enduring, marvelous authenticity of craftsmanship. Hesse writes, it seems to me, the most beautiful German being written today, whether his sentences are expressing a colorful lyricism or portraying a sparse and highly conscious simplicity of expression"

53 Above, Oskar Loerke (1884–1941) as a young man;
Hesse's future editor at S. Fischer Verlag, who, in 1904,
after reading *Peter Camenzind*, wrote in his diary: "A
very good book. I believe that it belongs to those which
will resound quietly for a long time": "Among the
strongest creative forces in the lyric, along
with Trakl and Benn, he was for decades a secret king
of modern avant-garde poetry, a much imitated pioneer,
an example and father of the best in his generation
and the following one." (Hesse, 1958, in reference to
Loerke)

54 Stefan Zweig (1881–1942), the Austrian novelist.
From February 1903 in correspondence with Hesse,
whom he visited for the first time in 1905 at Gaienhofen

55 Hesse's sons: Heiner (born 1909), Bruno (born 1905), and Martin (born 1911)

56 With his friend the writer Emil Strauss, in Bernrain near Emmishofen on Lake Constance

7. September 1912 — Preis 50 Pf.

März

Eine Wochenschrift

Gegründet von Albert Langen

Herausgeber:

Ludwig Thoma · Hermann Hesse

Aus dem Inhalt:

J. Fischer, Heilbronn, Eine Entscheidungsfrage für den Liberalismus

Hans Dominik, Elektrisches Fernsehen

Maxim Gorki, Klagen

Hermann Hesse, Gedichte von Bruno Frank

Theodor Heuß, Die Deutschen im amerikanischen Bürgerkriege

6. Jahrgang
Heft 36

März-Verlag
G.m.b.H.
München

57 In January 1907 appeared the first issue of the
liberal weekly *März*, which was directed against the
personal authority of Kaiser Wilhelm II. Until the end of
1912, Hesse served as co-editor, along with Ludwig
Thoma, the German novelist and satirist. From 1913 on,
Theodor Heuss was the editor of *März*. "I sought out
with Langen that poet's nook on Lake Constance
where two fine fellows—it is no exaggeration to say
the two finest—may be found. In Überlingen there
is Emil Strauss and in Gaienhofen Hermann Hesse.
. . . We want to bring together everybody in South
Germany who has knowledge and ability in politics,
literature, art, and scholarship." (Thoma, 1906, in a
letter to Conrad Haussmann)

58 Ludwig Thoma (1867–1921)

59 Left, the publisher Albert Langen (1869–1909). In 1906 he persuaded Hesse, whom he knew from his regular work for the satirical weekly *Simplicissimus*, to help edit the journal *März*. It was with his publishing house that *Gertrude*, Hesse's story of a musician, appeared in 1910

60 Conrad Haussmann (1857–1922), regular contributor to *März*, politician, a member of the Reichstag since 1890, Hesse's friend from 1908

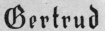

Gertrud

Roman
von
Hermann Heſſe

München, bei Albert Langen
1910

Unterwegs

Gedichte
von

Hermann Heſſe

Georg Müller Verlag
München
1911

61 Othmar Schoeck (1886–1957), one of the most important *Lieder* composers since Hugo Wolf; Hesse's friend since 1906. He composed the settings for twenty-three poems by Hesse: "I have endured, with shrugs or with horror, hundreds of settings for my poems. In Schoeck's settings there is nowhere the slightest misunderstanding of the text; nowhere is lacking the most delicate sense for nuances; and everywhere with almost startling certainty the finger touches the very center, the point where around a word or around the vibration between two words the experience of the poet has concentrated itself. He reads verse or sees pictures as a hunter reads the tracks of wild life." (Hesse, 1931)

62/63 Title pages of first editions of *Gertrude* and *On the Road*

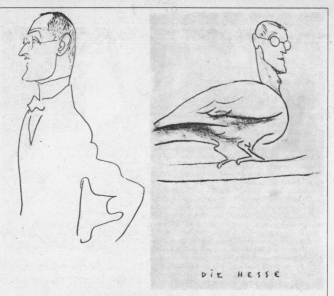

DIE HESSE

64/65 Caricatures of Hesse by Olaf Gulbransson. "The 'Hesse'—thus is named a delightful wood pigeon, which one no longer comes across in the wild. Because of its gracefulness it became a popular caged bird, and now regales the visitor by continuing to behave in its cage as though it were still in the open forest . . . it thereby provides the city dweller with a sensation of nature, which is enhanced by very small glands from which it secretes an aroma vaguely redolent of the fragrance of fir trees." (Franz Blei, *The Great Bestiary*)

66 Olaf Gulbransson (1873–1958), Norwegian painter and caricaturist; after 1902 illustrator for *Simplicissimus;* Hesse's friend

67 Thomas Mann, whom Hesse met in Munich in April
1904, through S. Fischer. Hesse reviewed the volume
of stories *Tristan* in 1903: "Thomas Mann is perhaps
the only one among our 'intellectuals' in *belles lettres* in
whom a great capacity for description is balanced by a
practiced skeptical reason. His novellas are not so much
tales as character studies." (Review, 1909)

Thomas Mann wrote about Hesse: "Of the literary
generation to which I belong I early chose him . . . as
the one nearest and dearest to me, and I have followed
his growth with a sympathy that sprang as much from
our differences as from our similarities"

68 The Stachus in Munich, around 1910. In the five
years of his editorial activity with the journal *März,*
Hesse often came to Munich, which he describes in
the tale *"Taedium vitae"*

Wer innerhalb gewisser Grenzen
Die edle Poesie betreibt,
Der ahnt oft nicht die Konsequenzen,
Die er auf sich herniederschreibt.

He who practices noble poetry
Within certain limits
Often does not suspect the consequences
That he calls down upon himself.

69/70 Hesse, around 1907, in Munich:

Wer seinen Dienst am Dienstag nie
Auf Donnerstag vertagt,
Der tut mir leid, er ahnt nicht wie
Der Mittwoch dann behagt.

He who never postpones his duty
From Tuesday to Thursday arouses my sympathy
For he has no idea
How marvelous Wednesday can be!

(Both poems from Hesse's unpublished light verse)

71 Hesse on the veranda of Am Erlenloh, his house in
Gaienhofen. A scissor-cut by Otto Blümel: "So
we were now prepared and settled for life . . . but
the eternity for which we had built [our house] did not
last very long. I had exhausted Gaienhofen. There was
no longer any life there for me. Now I frequently
went away for short periods and finally even journeyed
to India"

72 Wilhelm Raabe, major nineteenth-century German
novelist, whom Hesse visited in 1909 after a lecture in
Brunswick and described in the memoir "Visit to a
Writer"

"Literary history speaks of him with respect, is aware of him, has taken notice of him, but it has still failed to recognize the true miracle of his person and his language. Among his contemporaries Storm and Fontane are more securely and better classified in the literary histories than he. . . . But, as in the case of his predecessor Jean Paul, we found out that a writer over whom every university professor of literature for the past thirty years has turned up his nose can once again be decorated with all the wreaths of fame"

73/74 Hesse on the steamer *Prince Eitel Friedrich* (North German Lloyd Line) during his trip to India, Autumn 1911

On Hesse's right, his friend and traveling companion,
the painter Hans Sturzenegger.

"In 1911 I was in India, led there by the traditions of my father and grandfather. The teachings of the ancient Indians and Chinese had as much influence on me as the pietistically colored Christianity in my parents' home"

75 Hesse's trip to India. A shadow play produced by Otto Blümel. On the right, Hermann Hesse with butterfly net

76 The first edition of *Sketches from an Indian Journey*,
1913: "Among the peoples I saw were Malayans and
Javanese, Tamils, Singhalese, Japanese and Chinese.
About the latter there are only the greatest things to say:
an impressive people! The majority of the others are
the pathetic remains of an old paradise-people, who
have been corrupted and devoured by the West: dear,
good-natured, skillful, and talented people of nature
whom our culture is ruining. If the whites could better
endure the climate and let their children grow up here,
then there would be no more Indians." (Letter, November 1911)

BERN

On September 15, 1912, Hesse moved with his family to Bern.

77 View of the old city of Bern

78 The Junkerngasse with the cathedral of Bern

79 The house on Melchenbühlweg, formerly the resi-
dence of his friend Albert Welti, the painter. Hesse lived
in this house, "a neglected old aristocratic country es-
tate," until April 1919. The first work completed there
was the novel *Rosshalde*

80 Kurt Tucholsky, in correspondence with Hesse since
February 1913, wrote a favorable review of this novel
for the *Schaubühne*, a weekly magazine devoted to
theater arts

81 Kurt Tucholsky's inscription in the first edition of
his *Rheinsberg*. "It pleases me," wrote Hesse in 1932 to
Tucholsky, "that there is at least one other poet in
this troubled Germany whose mode of thinking and
literary-social standards are close to mine and congenial
to me. It pleases me no less that a gentleman of the press
writes these knowledgeable, conscientious, lucid, good
sentences and expresses thoughts that today are per-
ceived as well-nigh un-German since the reasonable
analysis of any matter is something that has become for
us almost as rare as a feeling for one's own language
and a sense of responsibility for it"

Herr Hermann Hesse
in herzliche Verehrung

Tucholsky.

Hermann Hesse
Roßhalde

S. Fischer/Verlag
BERLIN
1914

82 Hesse in the garden of the house in Bern, with his wife and his second son, Heiner

83 Cover design for the first edition of *Rosshalde*: "The unhappy marriage with which this book deals cannot be attributed to a wrong choice but rather, more profoundly, to the problem of an artist's marriage altogether. It poses the question whether a man who not only lives by instinct but wherever possible looks at life and portrays it objectively—whether such a man is even suited for marriage"

Karl Walser

Sechzehn

Steinzeichnungen

zu

Hermann Hesses

Knulp

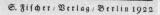

S. Fischer / Verlag / Berlin 1922

84 The story of the tramp Knulp originated between
1907 and 1914, partly in Gaienhofen and partly in
Bern. *Knulp* was first published in the magazine *Neue
Rundschau* in February 1908 and appeared as a book in
1915 as part of "Fischer's Library of Contemporary
Literature."

Karl Walser, brother of the novelist Robert Walser,
drew the first illustrations for *Knulp,* which appeared in
a limited edition of 360 signed copies in 1922.

Stefan Zweig wrote (October 1915) to Romain
Rolland: "Hesse's most recent book, *Knulp,* is to me his
loveliest; there is a Germany in it that no one knows,
not even we Germans, and that is truly lovable"

Feuilleton.

O Freunde, nicht diese Töne!
Von Hermann Hesse.

Die Völker liegen einander in den Haaren und jeden Tag leiden und sterben Ungezählte in furchtbaren Kämpfen. Mitten zwischen den aufregenden Nachrichten vom Kriegsschauplatz fiel mir, wie das so geht, ein längst vergessener Augenblick aus meinen Knabenjahren ein. Da saß ich, vierzehnjährig, an einem heißen Sommertag in Stuttgart in dem berühmten schwäbischen Landexamen, und als Aufsatzthema wurde uns diktiert: „Welche guten und welche schlechten Seiten der menschlichen Natur werden durch einen Krieg geweckt und entwickelt." Meine Arbeit über dies Thema beruhte auf keinerlei Erfahrung und fiel entsprechend traurig aus, und was ich damals, als Knabe, unter Krieg sowohl wie unter Kriegstugenden und Kriegslastern verstand, stimmt nicht mehr mit dem zusammen, was ich heute so nennen würde. Aber im Anschluß an die täglichen Ereignisse und an jene kleine Erinnerung habe ich dem Krieg in dieser Zeit viel nachgedacht, und da jetzt doch einmal der Brauch eingerissen ist, daß Männer der Studierstube und des Ateliers ihre Meinungen hierüber kundgeben, scheue ich mich nicht länger, auch die meine auszusprechen. Ich bin Deutscher und meine Sympathien und Wünsche gehören Deutschland, aber was ich sagen möchte, bezieht sich nicht auf Krieg und Politik, sondern auf die Stellung und Aufgaben der Neutralen. Damit meine ich nicht die politisch neutralen Völker, sondern alle diejenigen, die als Forscher, Lehrer, Künstler, Literaten am Werk des Friedens und der Menschheit arbeiten.

Da sind uns in letzter Zeit betrübende Zeichen einer unheilvollen Verwirrung des Denkens aufgefallen. Wir hören von Aufhebung der deutschen Patente in Rußland, von einem Boykott deutscher Musik in Frankreich, von einem ebensolchen Boykott gegen geistige Werke feindlicher Völker in Deutschland. Es sollen in sehr vielen deutschen Blättern künftig Werke von Engländern, Franzosen, Russen, Japanern nicht mehr übersetzt, nicht mehr anerkannt, nicht mehr kritisiert werden. Das ist kein Gerücht, sondern Tatsache und schon in die Praxis getreten.

Also ein schönes japanisches Märchen, ein guter französischer Roman, von einem Deutschen noch vor Kriegsbeginn treu und liebevoll übersetzt, muß jetzt totgeschwiegen werden. Eine schöne, gute Gabe, mit Liebe unserm Volke dargebracht, wird zurückgestoßen, weil einige japanische Schiffe Tsingtau bekriegen. Und wenn ich heute das Werk eines Italieners, eines Türken, eines Rumänen lobe, so darf das nur mit dem Vorbehalt gelten, daß nicht vor Beendigung des Abdrucks in diesen Völkern ein Diplomat oder Journalist die politische Lage ändert!

Anderseits sehen wir Künstler und Gelehrte mit Protesten gegen kriegführende Mächte auf den Plan treten. Als ob jetzt, wo die Welt in Brand steht, solche Worte vom Schreibtisch irgend einen Wert hätten. Als ob ein Künstler oder Literat, und sei er der beste und berühmteste, in den Dingen des Krieges irgend etwas zu sagen hätte. Als ob Heeresleiter in ihren Aktionen sich von solchen Worten beeinflussen lassen könnten und dürften.

85 Along with Karl Kraus, a Viennese satirist and social critic, and the novelists Heinrich Mann and Stefan Zweig, Hesse belonged to the diminishingly small number of German intellectuals who did not share the widespread war fever. "O Friends, Not These Sounds" was the first of numerous admonitions published by Hesse during the war years. Appeared November 3, 1914, in the newspaper *Neue Zürcher Zeitung*

86 Mobilization at the outbreak of World War I: "For almost ten years the protest against the war, against the raw, bloodthirsty stupidity of mankind, the protest against the 'intellectuals,' especially those who preached war, constituted for me a bitter necessity and duty." (Letter, circa 1930)

Jeder hats gehabt,
Keiner hats geschätzt,
Jeden hat der süße Quell gelabt,
O wie klingt ~~das~~ ~~[illegible]~~ Name
Friede jetzt!

Klingt so fern u. zag,
Klingt so tränenschwer,
Keiner weiß u. kennt den Tag,
Jeder sehnt ihn voll Verlangen her.

—

Sei willkommen einst,
Erste Friedensnacht,
Lieber Stern, wenn endlich du erscheinst
Ueberm Feuerdampf der letzten
Schlacht.

—

Dir entgegen blickt
Jede Nacht mein Traum,
Ungeduldig rege Hoffnung pflückt
Schauend schon die goldne Frucht vom Baum.

—

Sei willkommen einst,
Wenn aus Blut u. Not
Du am Erdenhimmel uns erscheinst,
Unserer schönen Zukunft Morgenrot!

—

Meinem lieben
Conrad Haußmann
von seinem H Hesse
Stuttgart 11. X. 1914.

87 First copy of the poem "Peace," which Hesse
inscribed in the guestbook of Conrad Haussmann in
Stuttgart

88 Hesse shortly before the outbreak of World War I

Ein neues Kapitel der Gefangenen-Fürsorge.

Bericht aus Davos

von

Hermann Hesse.

I.

Seit kurzem ist nun endlich der erste Anfang zur „Hospitalisierung" kranker Kriegsgefangener in der Schweiz gemacht. Der schöne und für die nächste Zukunft hoffentlich noch weiter wirkende Gedanke dazu ging vom Vatikan aus; es hat lange gedauert, bis zwischen Deutschland, Frankreich und der Schweiz die Verhandlungen so weit gediehen, daß der fruchtbare Gedanke zur Tat werden konnte.

An sich bedeutet die Unterbringung kranker Kriegsgefangener in Kurorten eines neutralen Landes einen entschiedenen Fortschritt in der Fürsorge für die Opfer des Krieges. Man hat seit 1½ Jahren oft genug sagen hören, mit der Humanität sei es jetzt für eine gute Weile vorbei, sie sei ein schönes Wort für Gefühlsselige geworden, hinter dem keine Wirklichkeit stehe. Kraftnaturen haben sich über den scheinbaren Bankrott jener „Gefühlsduseleien" und über die neue Einstellung der Völker auf Kraft, auf intensive Leistung und gesund-primitive Machtinstinkte gefreut, und zum Teil mit gutem Grunde, denn wirklich kann niemand sich der Einsicht verschließen, daß der große Appell an Männlichkeit und Kriegertugend für Ungezählte einen Ruf zur Genesung, zur Einkehr, zur Ermannung bedeutete.

89 Romain Rolland (1866–1944), in correspondence with Hesse from 1915–40. The correspondence commenced with a letter of thanks for Hesse's first antiwar essay

90 First of a series of articles in the newspaper *Der Tag*, in Berlin, on July 12 and 16, 1916. From September 1915 to April 1919 Hesse worked as a volunteer for the German Prisoner-of-War Welfare Organization in Bern, which provided over a half million prisoners and internees in France, England, Russia, and Italy with reading matter. Along with this, Hesse managed two newspapers for prisoners and edited a series of books for them

91 With his oldest son, Bruno, on the Schaafschnur
above Lake Öschinen, near Bern, in the summer of 1915

92 Cover of the first edition of *Along the Way*, eight
short prose pieces which were published in 1915 by
Reuss and Itta in Constance

From an early date Hesse repeatedly commented on
Robert Walser and Frank Kafka (right) in many
reviews and articles.

93 "If such writers as Walser belonged to the 'leading intellectuals' then there would be no war . . . a pure musician, which gives to all of his writings an art which has almost returned to nature, a virtuosity handled in a childlike and naïve manner"

94 "When most of the German literature which we now value is forgotten, people will still be reflecting on and discussing this pedantically precise visionary, who wrote such exemplary German and who was actually much more than a mere dreamer and writer"

95 Dr. Josef Bernhard Lang (1883–1945), a student
of Carl Gustav Jung, became Hesse's doctor in 1916.
Pistorius in the novel *Demian* is modeled after him.
(Etching by Gregor Rabinowitsch)

It was with Lang that Hesse sought treatment for a
nervous breakdown after "months of overwork" and
the sudden death of his father: "At the moment I feel
only the fading of impulses and modes of thought that
were once precious and lively and a growth of new
things that are still inchoate and that cause me more
anxiety than pleasure. This development has also been
accelerated by the terrible war, which has exerted
agonizing pressure." (Letter, 1916)

96 Hesse's father, shortly before his death on March 8,
1916: "On the way home after my father's burial I
suddenly collapsed completely. An almost unbearable
headache plagues me most, otherwise only weakness,
some dizziness, and feelings of anxiety," wrote Hesse in
March 1916 to his friend the graphic designer Otto
Blümel

97 Carl Gustav Jung (1875–1961), by 1919 in
correspondence with Hesse. In 1921, during the
continuing crisis of almost eighteen months between
the writing of the first and the second parts of
Siddhartha, Hesse underwent psychoanalytic treatment
with Jung

98 Inscription from C. G. Jung for Hesse in
Gestaltungen des Unbewussten, Rascher Verlag, 1950:
"To Herr H. Hesse. Presented by the author and editor
in memory of old times"

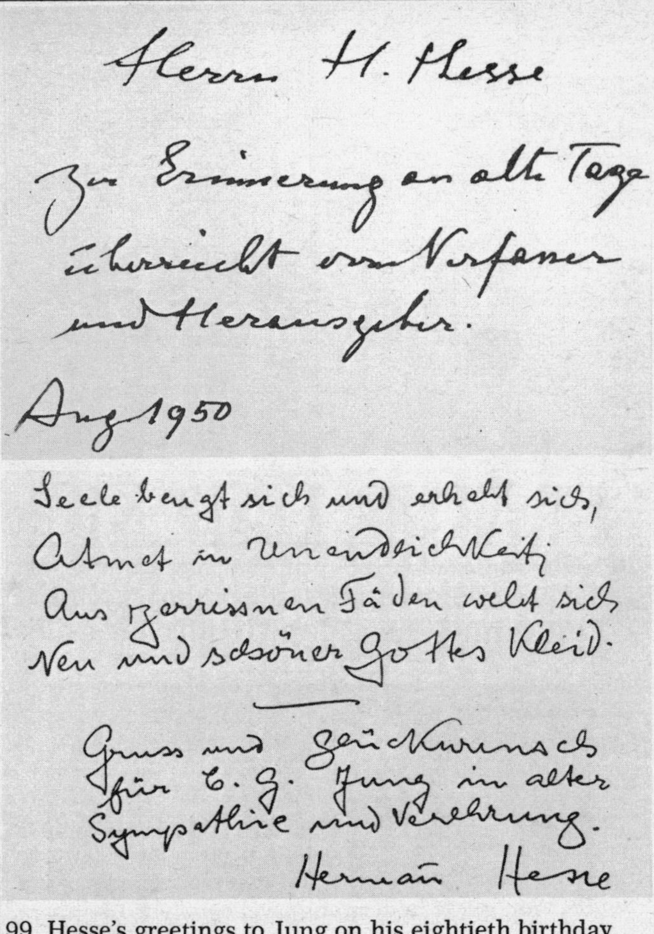

Herrn H. Hesse

Zur Erinnerung an alte Tage überreicht vom Verfasser und Herausgeber.

Aug 1950

Seele beugt sich und erhebt sich,
Atmet in Unendlichkeit;
Aus zerrissnen Fäden webt sich
Neu und schöner Gottes Kleid.

Gruss und Glückwunsch für C. G. Jung in alter Sympathie und Verehrung.

Hermann Hesse

99 Hesse's greetings to Jung on his eightieth birthday, July 26, 1955:

> The soul inclines and rises,
> Breathes in infinity;
> From broken threads is woven
> Anew and more beautifully God's raiment.

> Greetings and best wishes for C. G. Jung as a token of fondness and respect

Zarathustras
Wiederkehr

Ein Wort an die deutsche Jugend
Von einem Deutschen

BERN
Verlag von Stämpfli & Cie.
1919

Demian
die Geschichte einer Jugend

von

Emil Sinclair

O. Fischer Verlag
Berlin

100 First edition of the political pamphlet *Zarathustra's
Return,* which was published anonymously in 1919:
"We must not begin at the end with reforms of government and political methods, but rather we must start at
the beginning with the construction of the personality. If
we want once again to have minds and men who will
guarantee a future for us . . . we must plunge our roots
more deeply and not merely shake the branches"

101 First edition of *Demian,* which appeared in 1919
under the pseudonym "Emil Sinclair"

102 Illustration by Günther Böhmer for *Demian*

Csorbató 23. 8. 18.

Freud

103 Postcard from Sigmund Freud to Hesse, in which he
expresses appreciation for the article "Artists and
Psychoanalysis" which appeared in the *Frankfurter
Zeitung,* July 16, 1918

104 Sigmund Freud (1856–1939), whose work Hesse
had supported in reviews and articles from 1918 on:
"The beauty and remarkable charm in the writings of
Freud consist in the attraction of an extraordinarily
brilliant intellect to questions which all lead into the
suprarational, and in the continually renewed patience
and daring attempt to entrap life itself with the overly
coarse net of pure scientific method. As a careful
investigator and clear logician, Freud has created for
himself an excellent instrument in his wholly intellectual
but splendidly acute, precisely defining, occasionally
pugnacious and sarcastic language—how many of our
scholars can we say that about?" (Review, 1925)

„Vivos voco“.

Ein Dichter und ein Gelehrter, die seit Jahren gemeinsam in der Fürsorgearbeit tätig sind und dabei eine große Menge Elend kennen gelernt haben, versuchen auf ihre Weise zur Linderung der immer mehr wachsenden Not des deutschen Volkes beizutragen. Sie haben eine Zeitschrift gegründet, „Vivos voco“, die literarischen und politischen Ehrgeiz hat, die aber in den nächsten Jahren vorzugsweise dem dienen will, was die Herausgeber und Viele mit Ihnen als das zur Zeit Allerdringendste erkannt haben: der Fürsorge für die der Hilfe am meisten Bedürftigen, vor allem für die deutschen Kinder als die Träger unserer so schwer gefährdeten Zukunft.

Nicht nur soll der Ertrag der Zeitschrift der Kinderfürsorge zugute kommen, sondern sie will auch versuchen, über alle Bestrebungen auf dem weiten Gebiete der Fürsorge Auskunft zu geben und den Dilettantismus und Bürokratismus, der nirgends so schädlich hervortritt wie hier, nach Möglichkeit zu bekämpfen. Neben dem Kampf gegen Hunger und Krankheit unserer Kinder halten Hesse und Woltereck für die wichtigsten Tagesfragen die Jugendbewegung und Erziehungsreform. Diesen Fragen der körperlichen und der „geistigen“ Jugendfürsorge, von deren richtiger Behandlung nicht nur für Deutschland so ungeheuer viel abhängt, will die Zeitschrift ihre besondere Aufmerksamkeit widmen, ohne daß deshalb die künstlerischen und politischen Probleme vernachlässigt werden.

Die Ziele der Zeitschrift sind von den Herausgebern in kurzen Aufsätzen besprochen worden mit denen das 1. und 2. Quartal (Heft 1 und 4) eingeleitet werden. Außerdem sei auf die große Novelle von Hermann Hesse in den Heften 1—3 „Klein und Wagner“ hingewiesen. In dieser Arbeit tritt die große Wandlung, die Hesses Kunst unter der Einwirkung der letzten fünf Jahre erfahren hat, zum ersten Male deutlich hervor. Ferner erwähnen wir die literarischen Beiträge von Klabund und Sinclair, die programmatischen Aufsätze Wolterecks über die „Neue Jugend und die Führerschaft Deutschlands“, über „Kultursiedelungen“ und über „Geistige Nothilfe für Deutschland und Österreich“. Aufsätze von Eduard Spranger, Otto Flake, Prof. Kampfmeyer, Prof. Hildenbrand, Oberst Feldmann, u. a. behandeln verschiedene Gebiete der geistigen, politischen und wirtschaftlichen Reformen. Überdies enthält jedes Heft eine Auswahl von Notizen unter den vier ständigen Rubriken: „Aus der Fürsorgearbeit“, „Aus der Jugendbewegung und Erziehungsreform“, „Notizen zur Zeit“, „Aus der Literatur“. Die letztgenannte Rubrik, welche fast ausschließlich Buchbesprechungen aus der Feder Hermann Hesses enthält, wird die Leser der Zeitschrift besonders fesseln.

„Vivos voco“ erscheint monatlich im Kommissions-Verlage von Seemann & Co. in Leipzig und ist in der Schweiz durch die Buchhandlung A. Francke-Bern oder durch die Administration in Bern-Gümligen zu beziehen. Sie ist kein geschäftliches Unternehmen, sondern bildet ein Glied der deutschen Kinderfürsorge, der sie ihre Reineinnahmen zu überweisen hat.

105 Announcement of a new publication, the German monthly *Vivos Voco*, founded by Hesse and the biologist Richard Woltereck. Hesse served as co-editor until the end of 1921

106 Title page of *Vivos Voco*. First issue appeared in October 1919

107 One of the publications Hesse supervised as part of his welfare activity was *Christmas Calendar 1918 for the German Prisoners of War:* "I occupy myself again with work for the prisoners' Christmas and view the world theater with no more satisfaction than I did two or four years ago. Everybody in the world is stabbing and shooting away at one another. Nobody wants to acknowledge and concede and improve a shortcoming in himself—shooting is much easier." (Letter, August 1918)

108 *In Sight of Chaos: Two Essays on Dostoevsky and a Dialogue:* "It is still astonishing to me how much continuity all my work displays—from the *Zarathustra* pamphlet down to my last work on Dostoevsky—and how greatly it follows spontaneous and yet almost predestined paths." (Letter, 1919)

109 T. S. Eliot (1888–1965) visited Hesse in
Montagnola in May 1922 after reading *In Sight of
Chaos:* "I have become acquainted with *In Sight of
Chaos,* which I admire greatly. I find in your book
evidence of a serious concern which has not yet
penetrated to England, and I would like to spread its
reputation"

MONTAGNOLA

110 View from Montagnola of Lake Lugano
(photograph on overleaf)

111 In the so-called Parrots' House in Carona, which
is described in *Klingsor's Last Summer*

112 Casa Camuzzi in Montagnola, where Hesse lived
from May 1919 to August 1931 (Pen-and-ink drawing
by Hesse, upper right): "During that period [1919–
circa 1923], while my books were being translated into
twenty-five languages, I lived like a beggar"

113 View of the village of Montagnola

114 View from the terrace of Casa Camuzzi of "Klingsor's Garden": "The tile-covered ledge in the foreground belongs to the roof terrace of my first apartment in Montagnola. The tall house on the right with the stepped gable was my lodging at the time, and the small balcony on the top floor belonged to my study. *Klingsor* begins with this balcony." (Letter, 1956) (Ink and watercolor sketch by Hesse)

115 Klingsor's "narrow stone balcony" overlooking
the old terrace garden

116 Hesse sitting by the window of his study in
Casa Camuzzi, 1919

117 Souvenir snapshot of an outing in Carona. From
right to left: Hugo Ball, Emmy Ball-Hennings, Hesse,
and a friend

118 With Ruth Wenger (1920), whom Hesse married
in 1924. She is depicted in *Klingsor's Last Summer*.
"At night the moon raced as though mad across the sky,
soon it was morning again, and one crept home with a
belly full of red wine. We were also in Carona . . . the
elegant young lady Ruth ran about in a fire-red dress,
accompanied by an aunt, two dogs, and a piano tuner,
who unfortunately was insane. It was a splendid
menagerie. The whole thing ended in a dim grotto, which
was somewhere high, while down below brightly lit
trains whizzed past. We kissed women and tree trunks—
it was dreadfully beautiful." (Letter, 1919)

119 View from Hesse's window in the Casa Camuzzi

120 "During the summer months my main occupation
is not literature but painting. . . . I have my small
paint set in my hand; this is my magical apparatus and
Faustian cloak, with whose help I have practiced magic
a thousand times and won the battle against stupid
reality." (From *Aquarellen,* 1927)

121 Cover of the first edition of *Klingsor's Last Summer*, 1920

122 "Klingsor's Garden": "a deep, shadowed jumble of thick tree tops, palms, cedars, chestnuts, Judas tree, copper beech, eucalyptus, intertwined with climbing plants, vines, wisteria"

123 Ruth Wenger, Hesse's second wife

SIDDHARTHA

Eine indische Dichtung

von

Hermann Hesse

1 9 2 2

S. Fischer / Verlag / Berlin

124/125 Illustrations from the Indian edition of *Siddhartha*

126 Title page of the first edition. "*Siddhartha* is a very European book, despite its setting. The message of Siddhartha begins with the individual, which it takes much more seriously than any other Asiatic teaching. . . . *Siddhartha* is the expression of my liberation from Indian thinking. The pathway of my liberation from all dogma leads up to *Siddhartha* and will naturally continue as long as I live." (Letter, 1925)

"I sought to grasp what all religions and all human forms of piety have in common, what rises above all national differences, what can be believed by every race and every individual." (Preface to Persian edition, 1958)

127 "To my friend Hermann Hesse, the Samana, with fond memories." (Inscription by Romain Rolland in his book on Mahatma Gandhi, 1923)

128 Wilhelm Gundert (1880–1971). The first part of *Siddhartha* was published in the *Neue Rundschau* (July 1921) prior to its appearance in book form. This part was dedicated to Romain Rolland, the second to Wilhelm Gundert, Hesse's cousin and a specialist in Japanese culture

129 Richard Wilhelm (1873–1930), Sinologist and
translator of classical Chinese literature (Confucius,
Lao-tzu [Lao-tse], Chuang Tzu, Mencius, I Ching,
Li Chi, and Lieh Tzu): "He was a precursor and an
example, a man of harmony and of the synthesis
between East and West—between composure and
activity. He sought no escape from any European
problem, did not withdraw from any challenge of real
life, submitted neither to intellectual nor to aesthetic
quietism; but, step by step, he has effected in himself
the alliance and merging of the two great ancient ideals,
has reconciled within himself China and Europe, Yang
and Yin, thought and action, contemplation and
efficacy"

130 Hermann Hesse, about 1921, during the writing of
Siddhartha

131 Henry Miller (born 1891), who, in the early 1950's,
began to urge the translation of Hesse's books in the
United States. He wrote about his favorite book,
Siddhartha: "A book whose profundity is concealed in the
artfully simple and clear language, a clarity that
probably upsets the intellectual ossification of those
literary Philistines who always know so exactly what
good and bad literature is. To create a Buddha who
transcends the generally acknowledged Buddha is an
unheard-of achievement, especially for a German. For
me, *Siddhartha* is a more potent medicine than the
New Testament"

132 The spa hotel Verenahof in Baden near Zurich (the
Heiligenhof in *A Guest at the Spa*). Hesse went there
for several weeks at the end of each year for a cure
(1923–52), by invitation of Markwalder, the proprietor:
"It was there that the little book *A Guest at the Spa* had
its origin . . . stimulated partially by the
unaccustomed leisure of the spa and hotel life, partially
through sundry new acquaintances with people and
books, I found a mood of contemplation and
self-examination midway from Siddhartha to
Steppenwolf, an ironic and playful desire to observe
and analyze the transitory, a suspension between
sluggish indolence and intensive work." (*Notes on a
Cure in Baden,* 1949)

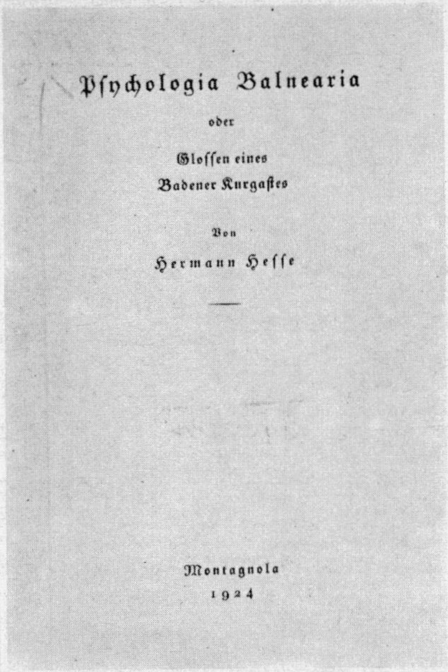

Pſychologia Balnearia

oder

Gloſſen eines
Badener Kurgaſtes

Von
Hermann Heſſe

Montagnola
1 9 2 4

133 Title page of the first edition of *A Guest at the Spa,*
which originally appeared in a private printing of
three hundred numbered copies. The trade edition
appeared a year later

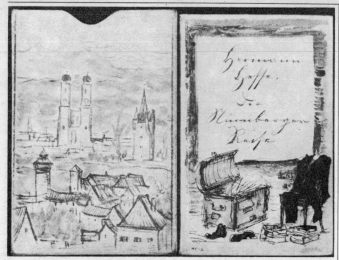

134 From 1905 to 1929, usually in the winter months,
Hesse took long trips in the German-speaking lands,
made possible by readings delivered in the large cities.
In September 1925 he went to Ulm, Augsburg, and
Nuremberg for readings, which he described in *The
Journey to Nuremberg* (1928)

135 Hesse, 1925

136 Klabund (1890–1928), Expressionist poet and novelist, acquainted with Hesse since 1920

137 Dedication in a copy of his *Travel Letters of an Artist*, 1926

138 Right, Joachim Ringelnatz (1883–1934), poet and cabaret performer, whom Hesse visited in Munich. Hesse portrayed him as the younger brother of Knulp, as Don Quixote, as "the young enthusiast with a poet's heart and a little bird in his knight's head, who derives pleasure from watching the play of his soap bubbles, a child and a sage in the midst of a goal-obsessed world of careerists and wage-earners"

An Hermann Hesse.

Nicht, daß ich dieses Buch dir schenke, – –
Nein, ich bedanke mich nur bei dir.
Und braucht doch kein Geburtstag sein,
daß deiner ich gedenke.

herzlichst
Joachim Ringelnatz.
Köln 13/14. 11. Sept. 27

Tractat

vom

Steppenwolf

Es war einmal einer namens Harry, genannt der Steppenwolf. Er ging auf zwei Beinen, trug Kleider und war ein Mensch, aber eigentlich war er doch eben ein Steppenwolf. Er hatte vieles von dem gelernt, was Menschen mit gutem Verstande lernen können, und war ein ziemlich kluger Mann. Was er aber nicht gelernt hatte, war dies: mit sich und seinem Leben zufrieden zu sein. Dies konnte er nicht, er war ein unzufriedener Mensch. Das kam wahrscheinlich daher, daß er im Grunde seines Herzens jederzeit wußte (oder zu wissen glaubte), daß er eigentlich gar kein Mensch, sondern ein Wolf aus der Steppe sei. Es mögen sich kluge Menschen darüber streiten, ob er nun wirklich ein Wolf war, ob er einmal, vielleicht schon vor seiner Geburt, aus einem Wolf in einen Menschen verzaubert worden war oder ob er als Mensch geboren, aber mit der Seele eines Steppenwolfes begabt und von ihr besessen war oder aber ob dieser Glaube, daß er eigentlich ein Wolf sei, bloß eine Einbildung oder Krankheit von ihm war. Zum Beispiel wäre es ja möglich, daß dieser Mensch etwa in seiner Kindheit wild und unbändig und unordentlich war, daß seine Erzieher versucht hatten, die Bestie in ihm totzukriegen, und ihm gerade dadurch die Einbildung und den Glauben schufen, daß er in der Tat eigentlich eine Bestie sei, nur mit einem dünnen Überzug von Erziehung und Menschentum darüber. Man könnte hierüber lang und unterhaltend sprechen und sogar Bücher darüber schreiben; dem Steppenwolf aber wäre damit nicht gedient, denn für ihn war es ganz einerlei, ob der Wolf in ihn hinein-

139 Hesse at the time of the composition of *Steppenwolf*. "If I should nevertheless someday write the book which I have in my head, the title would be *Only for Madmen* or *Anarchistic Evening Entertainment*." (Letter, 1924)

Steppenwolf, written from 1925 to 1927 in Basel, Montagnola, and Zurich, published in June 1927 by S. Fischer.

140 The tract from *Steppenwolf*: "Only for Madmen," in its original format in the first edition: "The garish yellow cover of the tract is my idea, and it was my special wish to emphasize forcefully the peculiar carnival-like character that the tract has in the story. The publisher was very much opposed for reasons of taste. I really had to be quite firm in order to prevail." (Letter, 1927)

141 Cover of the menu in the Hotel Baur au Lac
(Zurich) for the masked ball of the Municipal Art
Museum on February 6, 1926, which is described in
Steppenwolf

142 "Masked Ball." Watercolor by Hesse, 1926.
"While I lived like a young man of the world, danced a
lot, took part everywhere in the superficial pleasures
of the modern world which I had previously not known
at all and often found charming in their naïve
boisterousness—at the very same time I was constantly
concerned with the most serious problems that life
had given me. Thus, in the midst of all the turmoil, I
was intensely conscious and on the lookout as never
before." (Letter, 1926)

143 Hermann Hesse, 1927

144 Hugo Ball (1866–1927), dramatist, producer, Dadaist, writer; Hesse's friend since 1919. For Hesse's fiftieth birthday in 1927, Ball wrote a biography which today is still authoritative. "He never trifled with his unrelenting mockery of bourgeois, moral, and aesthetic conventions as well as with his fantastic-magical attempts to poeticize the stage and the artist's existence. He surrendered to it totally. But when things were underway, and Dadaism became an international fashion, the most significant of its founders was no longer involved. . . . During all those years we spoke about, discussed, and debated basically only one question: where is the point from which this complete hell of war, corruption, and de-spiritualization can be surveyed and overcome?" (Hesse, writing about Hugo Ball, 1930)

145 Lithograph by Alfred Zwinger for *Steppenwolf*, 1929

146 "MOZART: that means the world has a meaning, and
it is perceptible to us through the analogy of music."
(Diary, 1920/21)

"The majority of readers, especially those readers who
are not so young, find it [*Steppenwolf*] disconsolate and
despairing and believe that it deals with nothing but
the decline of our culture. But for anyone who can read,
it deals with just the opposite—the Eternal, Mozart,
and the Immortals." (Letter, 1930)

147 Kurt Pinthus (born 1889), senior editor of the
Rowohlt Publishing Company. He wrote in the Berlin
newspaper *8-Uhr Abendblatt* (July 2, 1927): "I am
reading *Steppenwolf*, this most merciless and
soul-searing of all confessional works, gloomier and
more unrestrained than Rousseau's *Confessions,* the
most gruesome birthday party that a writer has ever
celebrated with himself. . . . A genuinely German
book, grandiose and profound, psychological and
straightforward, an analytical novel of development
with romantic techniques, romantic complexities like
those found in most German novels and especially in
the novels of Hermann Hesse"

148 Hesse, 1927

Zu Johannes dem Täufer
sprach Hermann der Säufer:

Alles ist mir ganz willkommen,
Lass uns weiter schlendern!
So hat's seinen Lauf genommen,
Nichts ist mehr zu ändern.
Schau ich bin ein leeres Haus,
Tür und Fenster offen,
Geister taumeln ein und aus,
Alle sind besoffen.
Du hingegen hast noch Geld,
Zahl mir was zu trinken,
Voller Freuden ist die Welt,
Schade dass sie stinken!

Wer des Lebens Wonnen kennt,
Mag das Maul sich lecken,
Ausserdem ist uns vergönnt
Morgen zu verrecken.

ooooo

149 Manuscript of the poem "To John the Baptist from Hermann the Schnapps-ist." It first appeared in 1928 in *Krisis: Ein Stück Tagebuch* (*Crisis: Pages from a Diary*), which was issued in a limited edition of one thousand numbered copies: "Fischer would have agreed to publish it in a large edition, but I was opposed; for I consider this book a private affair. The time to make it a public matter will come only when I have been dead as long as Nietzsche today. One has to concede this to the Germans: even if they bitterly hate the mind and writers, after thirty to fifty years they are always able to determine whether the private affairs of a writer or philosopher were really only private or perhaps concerned everybody." (Letter, 1928)

150 Zurich, Schanzengraben 31. Here his friends, the
Leuthold family, had put a small apartment at his
disposal. Hesse spent the winters from 1925 to 1931
there: "More than half of all that I have written since
1925 was composed during those Zurich winters."
(Letter, 1932)

151 First edition of *Narcissus and Goldmund,* 1930:
"This story does not vie with reportage, does not concern
itself with contemporary reality, does not titillate us
with political matters, foolish goings-on, or racy tales, but
instead is—in the best sense of the word—Poetry,
timeless poetry." (Max Herrmann-Neisse)

152 The house in Montagnola which H. C. Bodmer had
built for Hesse in 1931. Hesse moved in in August
1931 (overleaf)

In November of the same year Hesse married the art
historian Ninon Dolbin (1895–1966), daughter of the
lawyer Dr. Jakob Ausländer from Czernowitz. Hesse had
been corresponding with her since 1909

153/154 Hermann Hesse and Ninon Dolbin shortly
after their first meeting

155–162 Titles which reflect Hesse's work as an editor.
A bibliography of the works edited or provided with
prefaces or afterwords by Hesse comprises seventy-five
different titles. "The concept of 'World Literature' that
Goethe conceived is most natural and indigenous to
[Hesse]. One of his writings even has that title: *A
Library of World Literature*. It is an example of vast
and devoted reading. . . . It is service, veneration,
selection, revision, presentation, and knowledgeable
advocacy—more than enough to fill the life of many a
learned *literatus*. But here it is a sheer excess of love
(and of energy!), an active hobby in addition to a
personal, extraordinarily personal, *opus*, which vainly
seeks its equal among contemporaries as far as levels
of interest and the problems of self and world are
concerned." (Thomas Mann)

Kurt Tucholsky on *A Library of World Literature*, in 1929:
"The way this little guide for putting together a library
is made is a real delight. It is totally subjective, and
only in that manner can anything approaching
objectivity be attained in this huge realm. Whoever is
guided by this little volume will profit from it. It towers
like a skyscraper above prevalent literary histories."

DIE IDEE

83 HOLZSCHNITTE

VON

FRANS MASEREEL

EINLEITUNG VON HERMANN HESSE

KURT WOLFF VERLAG / MÜNCHEN

Das

klassische Jahrhundert

deutschen Geistes

1750–1850

—

Herausgegeben

von

Hermann Hesse

—

Der Geist

der Romantik

—

Herausgegeben

von

Hermann Hesse

—

Erster Band

1925
Deutsche Verlags-Anstalt Stuttgart
Berlin und Leipzig

Design for the title pages of a projected twelve-volume
anthology, *The Classical Century of the German Spirit*.
(Manuscripts including Hesse's afterwords are among
his literary effects.) Owing to the publisher's negligence,
the edition never materialized.

Apart from the books that he edited, Hesse observed,
commented upon, and shaped the literary life of his age
with more than three thousand book reviews, which
from 1900 on were published in over sixty different
newspapers and periodicals.

163 Annette Kolb (1875–1967), German novelist and
essayist, Hesse's friend. Caricature by Olaf Gulbrannson

164 A portrait of Hesse by his friend Cuno Amiet
(1868–1961). Hesse wrote about Amiet (1919):
"His gaze transforms the world, draws the colors out of
the gray, senses the sun even in the twilight . . . he is
committed to no Thou-shalt and no program, but instead
does what his nature demands of him . . . all of his
paintings show an unforgettable something that is more
than mastery, an unremitting love, a captivation by the
magic of the world's colors"

165 Hesse in Montagnola

166 Bertolt Brecht, 1933, in Montagnola on his way to
visit Hesse (left to right: the writers Kurt Kläber and
B. von Brentano, Brecht, and another guest): "Once,
along with several others who had fled Germany, he
was with us for an afternoon. Among other matters,
we spoke about the burning of the books. I have enjoyed
and treasured his poems and tales from the beginnings
to today. His death is a great loss for me. He was the only
real writer among the German Communists and the only
one who still stood on the whole broad foundation of a
comprehensive literary education." (Letter, 1956)

Painters who were friends
of Hesse:

167 Alfred Kubin (1877–
1959): "In the midst of
our stupid entertainment
and art industry, he is one
of the few who I know are
hidden somewhere as
brothers and kindred
spirits, absorbed in their
games, but productive,
never corruptible, beyond
the swindles of everyday
life." (Hesse about Kubin,
1928)

168 Louis Moilliet (1880–1962), described as "Louis
the Gruesome" in *Klingsor's Last Summer* and in *Journey
to the East* as "one of the Swiss painters dearest to me."
(Letter, 1948)

169 Frans Masereel (1889–1972). Hesse wrote
introductions for Masareel's cycles of paintings *Die Idee
(The Idea)* and *Geschichte ohne Worte (Stories
without Words)*: "No other artist conveys the spirit
of life of our time as vigorously and comprehensibly
as he does." (Review, 1927)

170 Carl Hofer (1878–1955) often visited with Hesse
in Montagnola after 1920

171 Max Purrmann (1880–1966). After 1943, he lived
along with the painter Gunter Böhmer in the Casa
Camuzzi in Montagnola. Hesse dedicated his late poem
"The Old Painter in His Workshop" to him

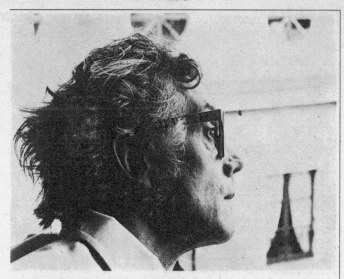

172 Gunter Böhmer (born 1911), painter and graphic
artist, professor at the Academy of Fine Arts in Stuttgart;
has lived in the Casa Camuzzi, Montagnola, since 1933:
"He is very gifted in all that pertains to graphics and
masters each technique easily. He is also a poetic, self-
absorbed man with a gift for storytelling." (Hesse, 1938)

173 Drawing of Hermann Hesse by Gunter Böhmer
(collection of Professor W. Jöhr, St. Gallen)

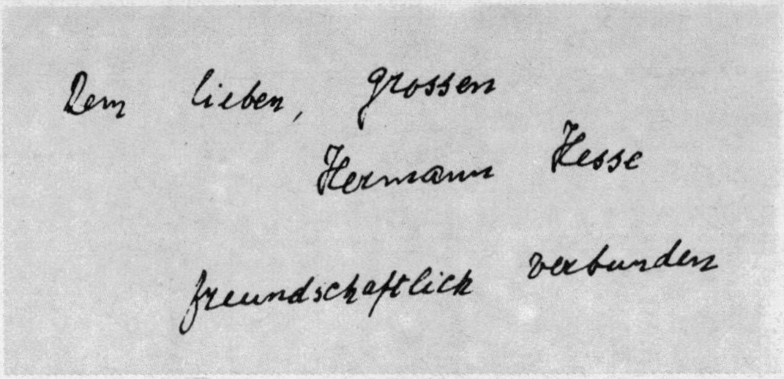

Dem lieben, grossen
Hermann Hesse
freundschaftlich verbunden

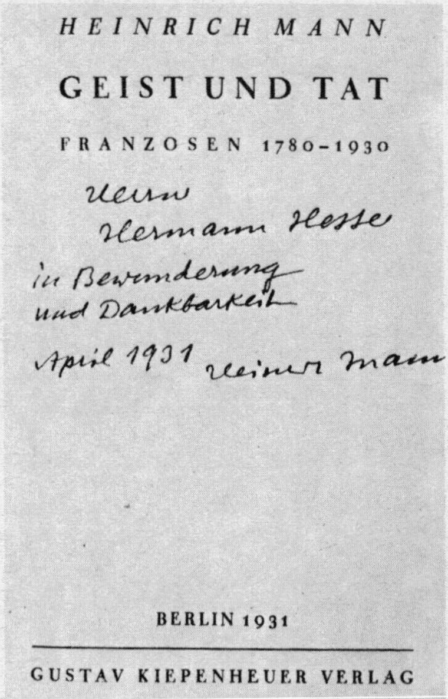

HEINRICH MANN

GEIST UND TAT

FRANZOSEN 1780–1930

Herrn
Hermann Hesse
in Bewunderung
und Dankbarkeit
April 1931   seiner Mann

BERLIN 1931

GUSTAV KIEPENHEUER VERLAG

174/175 Inscriptions in books from Thomas and
Heinrich Mann

176 Hesse with Thomas Mann and Jakob Wassermann
in Chantarella near St. Moritz, February 1932

177/178 With Thomas Mann in Chantarella, February
1932: "On that occasion my publisher, Fischer, was
there, along with Thomas Mann and Jakob Wassermann
and their families. We were suddenly famous people and
became acquainted with everyone. Since there was no
end to the introductions, it was really very stupid. . . .
Sometimes in the evening I sneaked away from the
ceremonious literary discussions into the playroom of
[Thomas Mann's] children." (Letter, 1932)

HERMANN HESSE

DIE MORGENLANDFAHRT

EINE ERZÄHLUNG

S. FISCHER VERLAG / BERLIN

179 André Gide (1869–1951). Since 1905 Hesse had
promoted his works in reviews and essays. Gide wrote an
introductory essay for the French edition of *Journey
to the East* (1948) in which he said: "The entire work
of Hesse is a poetic effort for emancipation with a
view to escaping imitation and reassuming the
genuineness which had been compromised. . . . Those
in his country who were able to remain loyal to
themselves, and not to allow themselves to be deflected
are rare. . . . With them we can come to an
understanding. With them we should speak."

180 First edition of *Journey to the East,* 1932, with dust
jacket, cover, and title vignette designed by Alfred Kubin

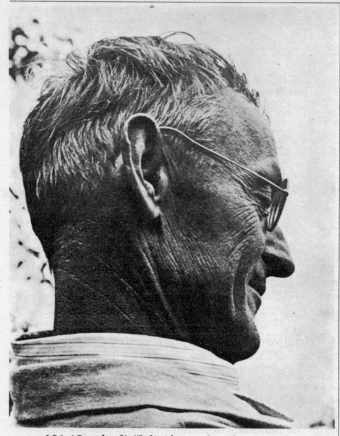

181 (Overleaf) "I divide my days between the study and garden work, the latter is intended for meditation and spiritual digestion and thus is usually undertaken in solitude." (Letter, 1934)

182 Hesse at the time of the writing of *The Glass Bead Game*

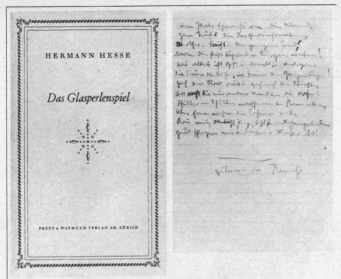

183 Cover of the first edition of *The Glass Bead Game*, which appeared in 1943 in Switzerland since publication was not permitted in Germany

184 Handwritten draft of the poem "Hurl Plato Against the Wall," from the preliminary studies for *The Glass Bead Game*. "The man of spirit should by no means sit at the tables of the wealthy and share in their luxury; he should be more or less an ascetic—however, he should not be ridiculed for his asceticism but respected for it. The minimum of material things should be provided for him automatically just as, for instance, in the time of monastic culture, a brother of the order, though forbidden to own personal possessions, could still live, and, in proportion to his achievements, share in the renown and authority of his order. The order of the spirit in life must not constitute any real aristocracy. An aristocracy is based on inheritance, and the spirit is not physically inheritable. Instead, any good order of spiritual life constitutes an oligarchy of the most spiritually endowed men; all means of cultivation are accessible to every gifted person." (Letter about *The Glass Bead Game*, 1935)

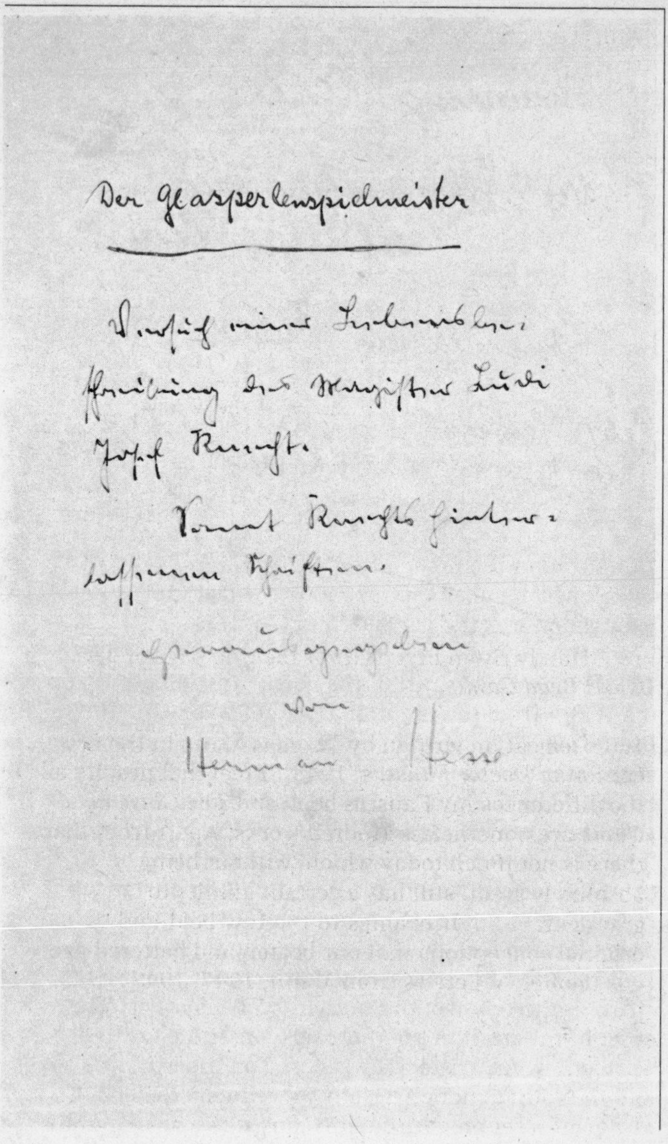

Der Glasperlenspielmeister

Versuch einer Lebensbe-
schreibung des Magister Ludi
Josef Knecht.

Samt Knechts hinterlas-
senen Schriften.

Herausgegeben
von
Hermann Hesse

Hermann Hesse

dies Glasperlenspiel mit
schwarzen Perlen

von seinem Freunde

Pacif. Palisades
15. Jan. 1948   *Thomas Mann*

185 Handwritten first draft of the title page of *The Glass Bead Game*

186 Dedication written by Thomas Mann in the first edition of *Doctor Faustus*, 1948. "I feel that despite all the differences my Faustus book and *The Glass Bead Game* are nonetheless kindred works. Apart from them there is not much today which, without being absolutely great, still has a certain affinity to grandeur. . . . It belongs to the few bold and original conceptions that our beaten and battered age has to offer." (Letters from Mann, 1947, 1948)

187 About 1943 in Baden

188 In conversation: "In the course of my career I
have never withdrawn from the problems of the
times and never, as my political critics have accused
me, lived in an ivory tower. But the first and most
consuming of my problems was never the state,
society, or the Church but instead the individual human
being, the personality—the unique individual who
has not been reduced to a norm." (Letter, 1951)

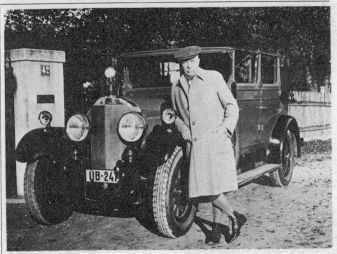

From above left:

189 Edwin Fischer (1886–1960), who composed music for Hesse's Elisabeth-poems: "For me Edwin was the man who, more than any other virtuoso, brought two of Beethoven's concertos close to me and even several pieces by Chopin, whose works I had once known very well . . . and he performed for me his *Lieder*, in which the atmosphere of the verses to Elisabeth had been perfectly attuned to a chromatics and a filigree technique derived from Chopin"

190 Justus Hermann Wetzel (born 1879), composer, who wrote settings for many Hesse poems (etching by Gunter Böhmer)

191 Richard Strauss (1864–1949). Among his last compositions are the settings for three poems by Hesse (in *Four Last Songs*)

192 Gottfried von Einem (born 1918) corresponded with Hesse and in 1973 composed a *Lieder* cycle based on poems by Hesse

193 The Nobel Prize for Literature was bestowed on
Hesse in 1946. In part, the citation read:
"Events have demonstrated through their development
that henceforth he can be considered along with Thomas
Mann as the most worthy custodian of the German
cultural heritage within contemporary literature."
Thomas Mann wrote to Frederik Bööks (1933/34):
"A long time ago I delivered my vote for Hermann Hesse,
the author of *Steppenwolf* . . . by choosing him, you
would honor Switzerland along with that older Germany
that is true, pure, spiritual and eternal. The world would
no doubt understand this, and even Germany, which
today is suffering in silence, would thank you from
the bottom of its heart"

194 Hesse in his library

195 At his desk. "Everywhere on earth there are people of our kind. That for a small part of them, I can be a focal point, the nodal point in the net, is the burden and the joy of my life." (Letter, 1955)

"The artist compensates for certain shortcomings in social behavior through his work. What he sacrifices for the sake of his work—and this is generally infinitely much more than what the nice average citizen would be capable of sacrificing—benefits everybody." (Letter, 1961)

196 With his wife Ninon

197 The worktable in his study, where Hesse prepared
his letters and packages for mailing—a task which
he performed himself without assistance until his death

198 View from the library to the dining room

199 With Bruno, his oldest son, after gardening

200 Robert Neumann, the novelist and playwright
(born 1897), wrote about Hesse: "It is time for
someone finally to straighten out our critics, among
whom in recent years it has become fashionable to
deny that Hesse has any good qualities at all. . . .
Even in Heine's *opus*, alongside the isolated passages of
greatness, there is a chaos of vapid singsong. Even in
Goethe's work. Six Hesse poems for the enduring body of
German lyric poetry—that is quite a bit for a single life.
And that these six poems will belong to this body—at a
time when the names of his critics will be found only in
the registers of deceased German high school teachers—
of this I am convinced." (1960)

201 Peter Weiss (born 1916) wrote in a letter to Hesse
in July 1962: "Twenty-five years ago I wrote to you
for the first time from Warnsdorf. At that time I was
at the beginning of my career. The letter with your
answer was a trailmark for me. Your personality and
your work had great significance for my development.
In all the stages of emigration, of dislocation, the war
years, until this very day I have carried your books
around with me"

202 Hesse bust by Hermann Hubacher (born 1885),
who was a close friend of Hesse

203 "Hesse as Gardener." Caricature by H. U. Steger.
"We are not masters of our appearance and the effects
that it produces. Therefore, I maintain the same position
of neutrality toward pictures of this sort that I maintain
toward the effects and side effects produced by my
books. Books, articles about me, illustrations, musical
settings for my poems—in all these matters I maintain
the same position: I let everyone do and say what they
want and feel no need to correct them." (Letter, circa
1950)

204 Ninon Hesse with Theodor Heuss in the Paulskirche
in Frankfurt in 1955, when the Peace Prize of the
German Booksellers' Association was bestowed on
Hesse. On the right, Richard Benz, German cultural
historian who gave the keynote address

205 Martin Buber (1878–1965) during his address in
Stuttgart on the occasion of the eightieth birthday of
Hermann Hesse: "Hermann Hesse, in his capacity as
writer, has served the spirit by telling of the conflict
between spirit and life and of the struggle of the
spirit against itself. Thereby he has rendered more
tangible the obstacle-ridden road that can lead to
a new wholeness and unity. . . . Wherever the spirit
is served, you are loved"

206 Hesse in 1955

207 With Theodor Heuss in Sils Maria in 1957.
"At a time in which the separate sectors of life broke
apart in unrestrained autonomy as never before, his work
rendered visible and credible the possibilities of a
harmony of man, world, and nature. Occidental spirit
and Oriental meditation come together in a higher unity
in a proclamation which belongs to the great hopes of
our day." (Heuss about Hesse, 1962)

HERMANN
HESSE
SPÄTE
PROSA

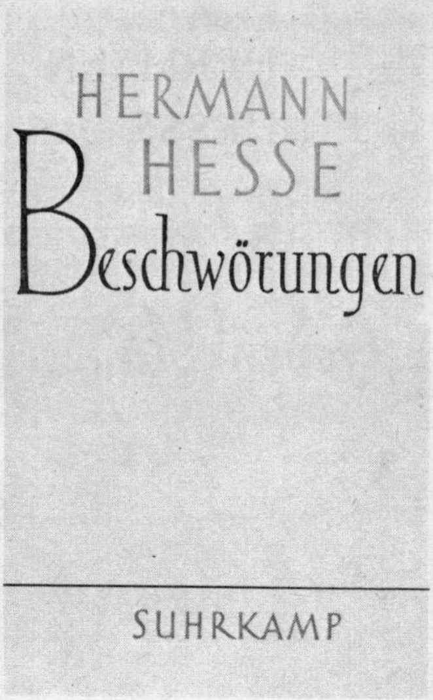

HERMANN
HESSE
Beschwörungen

SUHRKAMP

HERMANN
HESSE

Gedenkblätter

SUHRKAMP

208–210 The last volumes of prose that appeared during
Hesse's lifetime: *Late Prose* (1950), *Conjurations*
(1951), and *In Memoriam* (1956): "As in all my
commemorative writings, I was concerned not only
with the truth but much more with preserving
through language, as faithfully as possible, the
transitory and ephemeral. This is a rather Don Quixote–
like battle against death, against submersion and
oblivion." (Letter, 1953)

211 Hesse with David, his youngest grandson, in 1957

212 Resting during a walk near Carona: "I have
often sung the song of these mountains, forests,
vine-covered terraces, and lake valleys. Also that small
balcony in Klingsor's dwelling and that tall Judas tree
. . . have been described and praised. I have consumed
hundreds of sheets of paper and many tubes of color
in order to pay my respects with watercolors or ink
sketches to the old houses and tiled roofs, the garden
walls, the forests of chestnut trees, the mountains, far
and near"

213 Hesse, 1958

214 Theodor Heuss with Peter Suhrkamp, Hesse's
publisher, and his successor, Siegfried Unseld, at the
Book Fair in Frankfurt am Main (1957): "The
publisher must 'go with the times,' as one says. But
he must not simply accept the fashions of the time;
rather, when they are unworthy, he must be able to
resist them. The function of a good publisher, his very
inhalation and exhalation, is accomplished through
adaptability and critical resistance. You shall be like
that." (Letter to Siegfried Unseld from Hesse after the
death of Suhrkamp in 1959)

Kleiner Knabe

Hat man mich gestraft,
Halt ich meinen Mund,
Weine mich in Schlaf,
Wache auf gesund.

Hat man mich gestraft,
Heisst man mich den Kleinen,
Will ich nicht mehr weinen,
Lache mich in Schlaf.

Grosse Leute sterben,
Onkel, grosspapa,
Aber ich, ich bleibe
Immer, immer da.

HH. IV. 60

215 A late poem by Hesse, "The Little Boy." "Where art is concerned, I know that, just as in any time in the past, every true poem or painting, every measure of true music is paid for in equal measure with life, with suffering, with blood. Nothing has changed in the world except that which has always been on the surface and easily mutable: public opinion and moral standards. Fortunately, the serious worker can protect himself against these completely: it takes a little denial and asceticism, but it is very worthwhile." (Letter, 1932)

216 Watercolor and ink drawing by Hesse to illustrate his last poem, completed on the evening before his death

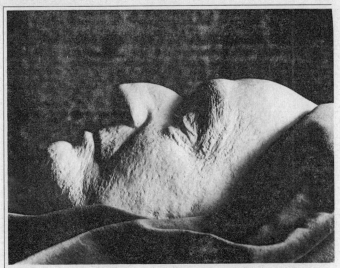

217 A late photograph of Hesse. "In reality, youth
and age exist only among ordinary people; all more
talented and exceptional people are sometimes young
and sometimes old, just as they are sometimes happy
and sometimes sad." (Letter, 1951)

"The goal of all literary endeavors is to appear in the
evening of life as Hermann Hesse does today. . . .
Within the guild of my fellow writers, I honor Hermann
Hesse the most." (Ernst Penzoldt, sculptor and writer)

218 Hesse's death mask: "The call of death is a call of
love. Death can be sweet if we answer it in the
affirmative, if we accept it as one of the great eternal
forms of life and transformation." (Letter, 1950)

219 The grave of Hermann Hesse and Ninon Hesse:
"Grief and lamentation are our first, natural response to
the loss of a beloved person. They help us through the
first mourning and loss, but they do not suffice to link us
with the deceased. That is done on the primitive level
by the cult of death: the sacrifices, grave decorations,
monuments, flowers. On our level, however, the sacrifice
must take place in our own souls through memory,
through the most detailed recollection, the reconstruction
of the beloved's being within our own. If we are able to
accomplish that, then the deceased remains close to us,
his image is preserved and helps us to make grief
productive." (Letter)

220 The cemetery at San Abbondio

ILLUSTRATION CREDITS

Fritz Eschen, Berlin-Wilmersdorf, 1

H. Fuchs, Calw, 2, 6, 8, 10

Schiller-Nationalmuseum, Marbach, 3, 5, 14, 20, 23, 26, 28, 31, 32, 33, 36, 38, 42, 43, 44, 46, 53, 58, 60, 73, 79, 81, 89, 98, 99, 103, 105, 106, 108, 111, 112, 114, 116, 117, 118, 119, 120, 121, 122, 123, 124, 127, 132, 133, 134, 137, 138, 144, 145, 147, 151, 168, 169, 171, 174, 175, 176, 179, 180, 184, 186, 187, 193, 203

Sammlung Eleonore Vondenhoff, Frankfurt am Main, 4, 11, 12, 17, 18, 19, 177

Bildarchiv des Suhrkamp Verlags, Frankfurt am Main, 7, 13, 16, 21, 29, 30, 76, 83, 84, 85, 86, 90, 92, 100, 101, 107, 109, 115, 125, 126, 140, 141, 142, 146, 149, 150, 155, 156, 157, 158, 159, 160, 161, 162, 164, 183, 185, 201, 208, 209, 210, 216

Aus Privatbesitz, 9, 25, 35, 48, 56, 72, 74, 128, 154, 166, 178, 196, 205, 215, 219, 220

Kurt Ziegler, Calw, 15

Württembergische Landesbibliothek, Stuttgart, 22

Landesbildstelle Württemberg, 24

J. J. Heckenhauer, Tübingen, 27

Stadtarchiv, Basel, 34

Bildarchiv des Fischer Verlags, Frankfurt am Main, 37, 94, 104

dpa, Frankfurt am Main, 39, 66, 97, 131, 167, 170, 189, 191, 192, 200, 204

Martin Hesse, Bern, 45, 69, 70, 77, 78, 82, 88, 91, 110, 113, 130, 135, 139, 143, 148, 152, 153, 165, 181, 182, 188, 194, 195, 199, 202, 206, 212, 213, 217, 218

Bundesbildstelle, Bonn, 52

Heiner und Isa Hesse, Küsnacht, 55, 95, 96, 197, 198, 211

Stadtarchiv, München, 59, 68

Hilde Schoeck, Zürich, 61

Dagny Gulbransson, Tegernsee, 64, 65, 163

Historisches Bildarchiv, Lolo Handtke, Bad Berneck, 67

Zentralbibliothek, Zürich, 71, 75

Kurt-Tucholsky-Archiv, Rottach-Egern, 80

Hauptstaatsarchiv, Stuttgart, 87

Jochen Greven, Frankfurt am Main, 93

Prof. Gunter Böhmer, Stuttgart, 102, 172, 173, 190

Bildarchiv des Eugen Diederichs Verlags, Köln, 129

Archiv Gescher-Ringelnatz, Berlin, 136

Diogenes Verlag, Zürich, 203

Pedrett, St. Moritz, 207

Lutz Kleinhans, Frankfurt am Main, 214

CHRONOLOGY

1877	Born July 2 in Calw in Württemberg. Son of Johannes Hesse (1847–1916), Baltic-born missionary and later director of the Calw Publishing House, and Marie Hesse (1842–1902), widow of Karl Isenberg, née Gundert, the oldest daughter of the missionary and well-known scholar of Indic languages and cultures Hermann Gundert.
1881–6	Hesse lived with his parents in Basel, where his father taught at the Basel Mission School. In 1883, his father, born a Russian citizen, was granted Swiss citizenship.
1886–9	Return to Calw, where Hesse attended elementary school.
1890–1	Attended the Latin school in Göppingen, in order to prepare himself for the Württemberg regional examinations (July 1891). To qualify he had to renounce his Swiss citizenship, and so in November 1890 his father obtained citizenship from Württemberg for him.
1891–2	Student at the seminary in Maulbronn (September 1891), from which he fled after seven months, because he "wanted to be either a writer or nothing at all" (April 1892).
1892	Stayed with Christoph Blumhardt for treatment with exorcism in Bad Boll (April-May). Attempted suicide (June). Sojourn in the clinic for nervous diseases at Stetten (June-August). Admitted to the Gymnasium in Cannstatt (November 1892).
1893	In July passed the selective-service examination as a qualification for one year's service as a volunteer. "Will become a Social Democrat and sit around in the cafés. Read almost only Heine, whom I have imitated a great deal."
1894–5	Apprentice in Perrot's Clockworks Factory in Calw.

1895–8	Apprentice in J. J. Heckenhauer's Bookshop in Tübingen.
1899	Began writing a novel, *Schweinigel* (*The Hedgehog*), the manuscript of which has disappeared. *Romantic Songs* (*Romantische Lieder*). *An Hour Beyond Midnight* (*Stunde hinter Mitternacht*).
1899–1903	Employed as stock clerk in Basel (R. Reich Bookdealers and Wattenwyl's Rare Books). Hesse began to write articles and reviews for the *Allgemeine Schweizer Zeitung*, which, more than his books, gave him "a certain local reputation that greatly improved his standing in society."
1901	First Italian journey: to Florence, Genoa, Pisa, Venice. *Hermann Lauscher*.
1902	*Poems* (*Gedichte*), dedicated to his mother, who died shortly before publication of the small book.
1903	Second journey to Italy—to Florence and Venice—in connection with his profession as a bookdealer. Finished the composition of *Peter Camenzind*, which he sent to Berlin at the invitation of S. Fischer Publishers.
1904	*Peter Camenzind.* Married Maria Bernoulli, member of an old Basel academic family. Moved in July to a vacant peasant house in Gaienhofen on Lake Constance. Began career as free-lance writer and contributor to numerous newspapers and journals (among others, *Die Propyläen*, the Munich newspaper; *Die Rheinlande; Simplicissimus; Der Schwabenspiegel*, the Württemberg newspaper). *Boccaccio.* *Francis of Assisi* (*Franz von Assisi*).
1905	Birth of his first son, Bruno.
1906	*Beneath the Wheel* (*Unterm Rad*), which Hesse had begun in 1903–4. Founding of *März*, a liberal weekly directed against the personal authority of Kaiser Wilhelm II. Hesse continued as co-editor until 1912.

1907	*In This World (Diesseits)*. In Gaienhofen, Hesse had a house of his own built and moved into it: Am Erlenloh.
1908	*Neighbors (Nachbarn)*.
1909	Birth of his second son, Heiner.
1910	*Gertrude (Gertrud)*.
1911	*On the Road (Unterwegs)*, poems. Birth of his third son, Martin. Journey to India with his friend Hans Sturzenegger, the artist.
1912	*Detours (Umwege)*, stories. Hesse left Germany and moved with his family to Bern, where he lived in the former residence of his friend Albert Welti, the artist.
1913	*Sketches from an Indian Journey (Aus Indien)*.
1914	*Rosshalde*. When the war began, Hesse reported for duty voluntarily. Deferred when found unfit for military service and assigned to the embassy in Bern. Edited and managed newspapers for German prisoners of war. Established a separate publishing company for prisoners of war (called the Publisher of the Book Center for German Prisoners of War), through which twenty-two volumes appeared from 1918 to 1919.
1914–19	Numerous political articles, admonitions, open letters appeared in German, Swiss, and Austrian newspapers.
1915	*Knulp* (prepublication in 1908). *Along the Way (Am Weg)*. *Music of the Lonely (Musik der Einsamen)*, poems. *Youth, Beautiful Youth (Schön ist die Jugend)*. Death of his father, illness of his wife and his youngest son, Martin, led to a nervous breakdown. First psychotherapy with J. B. Lang, student of C. G. Jung, in Sonnmatt near Lucerne.
1919	Political pamphlet *Zarathustra's Return (Zarathustras Wiederkehr)* published anon-

ymously. (Later, with the author's name, 1920.)

Moved to Montagnola, Ticino, where he lived in the Casa Camuzzi until 1931.

Little Garden (*Kleiner Garten*).

Demian, published under the pseudonym Emil Sinclair.

Strange News from Another Star (*Märchen*).

Founder and editor of the monthly *Vivos Voco.*

1920   *Poems of the Painter* (*Gedichte des Malers*), ten poems with sketches in color.

Klingsor's Last Summer (*Klingsor's letzter Sommer*).

Wandering (*Wanderung*).

1921   *In Sight of Chaos* (*Blick ins Chaos*).

Selected Poems (*Ausgewählte Gedichte*).

Crisis with almost eighteen months of unproductivity between the writing of the first and second parts of *Siddhartha.*

Psychoanalysis with C. G. Jung in Küsnacht near Zurich.

Eleven Watercolors of Ticino (*Elf Aquarelle aus dem Tessin*).

1922   *Siddhartha.*

1923   *Sinclair's Notebook* (*Sinclairs Notizbuch*).

First sojourn at the spa in Baden near Zurich.

1924   Hesse became a Swiss citizen again.

Married Ruth Wenger, daughter of the writer Lisa Wenger.

A Guest at the Spa (*Kurgast;* private printing); appeared a year later as the first volume of his *Collected Works.*

1925   *A Guest at the Spa.*

1926   *Picture Book* (*Bilderbuch*).

Elected a member of the Prussian Academy of Writers (poetry section). He resigned from it in 1931: "I have the feeling that during the next war this academy will contribute quite a few names to the group of those ninety or one hundred prominent men who again, just as in 1914, will de-

ceive the people about all important questions at the bidding of the state."

1927   *The Journey to Nuremberg* (*Die Nürnber-
ger Reise*).
Steppenwolf.
Hesse biography by Hugo Ball published
for Hesse's fiftieth birthday.
At the request of his second wife, Ruth, a
divorce was granted.

1928   *Reflections* (*Betrachtungen*).
Crisis: Pages from a Diary (*Krisis: Ein
Stück Tagebuch*).

1929   *Consolation of the Night* (*Trost der
Nacht*), poems.
A Library of World Literature (*Eine Bi-
bliothek der Weltliteratur*).

1930   *Narcissus and Goldmund* (*Narziss und
Goldmund*).

1931   Married Ninon Dolbin, née Ausländer, an
art historian. Moved into the house on the
Collina d'Oro in Montagnola built by
H. C. Bodmer for Hesse, with lifetime right
of occupancy.
The Inward Way (*Weg nach Innen*), four
stories (*Siddhartha, Soul of a Child, Klein
and Wagner, Klingsor's Last Summer*).

1932   *Journey to the East* (*Die Morgenlandfahrt*).

1932–43   Composition of *The Glass Bead Game*
(*Glasperlenspiel*).

1933   *Little World* (*Kleine Welt*), stories from
Neighbors, Detours, and *Sketches from an
Indian Journey,* slightly revised.

1934   *From the Tree of Life* (*Vom Baum des
Lebens*), selected poems.

1935   *Storybook* (*Fabulierbuch*).

1936   *Hours in the Garden* (*Stunden im Garten*).

1937   *In Memoriam* (*Gedenkblätter*).
New Poems (*Neue Gedichte*).
The Lame Boy (*Der lahme Knabe*).

1939–45   Hesse's works were proscribed in Germany.
*Steppenwolf, Reflections, Narcissus and
Goldmund* could no longer be printed. In
all, during the years 1933–45, twenty titles

by Hesse (including reprints) were available, and in those twelve years they reached a total of 481,000 copies (a number somewhat below the number of Hesse books sold in German-speaking countries in 1972 alone). To be sure, 250,000 of these copies may be accounted for by the Reclam volume *In the Old Sun* (1943) and a further 70,000 by the selection of poems *From the Tree of Life*, which appeared in 1934 in the series *Insel-Bücherei*. Nevertheless, the publication of the *Collected Works in Separate Volumes* continued in Switzerland with Fretz and Wasmuth Publishers.

1942   *Poems (Die Gedichte)*, the first complete edition of Hesse's poetry.

1943   *The Glass Bead Game.*

1945   *The Flowering Branch (Der Blütenzweig)*, a selection from the poems.
Bertold.
Dream Traces (Traumfährte).

1946   *If the War Goes On . . . (Krieg und Frieden).*
Publication of Hesse's works was resumed in Germany by Suhrkamp Publishing Company (formerly S. Fischer).
Goethe Prize awarded by Frankfurt am Main.
Nobel Prize.

1951   *Late Prose (Späte Prosa).*
Letters (Briefe).

1952   *Collected Works* in six volumes (*Gesammelte Dichtungen*). Special edition for the author's seventy-fifth birthday.

1954   *Piktor's Metamorphoses (Piktors Verwandlungen)*. Facsimile edition.
The Correspondence of Hermann Hesse and Romain Rolland (Briefe: Hermann Hesse–Romain Rolland).

1955   *Conjurations (Beschwörungen). Late Prose/New Series (Späte Prosa/Neue Folge).*
Peace Prize of the German Booksellers' Association.

1956	Establishment of a Hermann Hesse Prize by the Society for the Advancement of German Art in Baden-Württemberg.
1957	*Collected Works* in seven volumes (*Gesammelte Schriften*).
1961	*Steps* (*Stufen*), a selection of old and new poetry.
1962	*In Memoriam* (*Gedenkblätter*). (The 1937 edition expanded to include fifteen additional texts.) August 9—the death of Hermann Hesse in Montagnola.

INDEX